St. Brigid of Ireland

In memory of a happy
visit to Good Counsel
College

Alice Curtayne
3 —— III —— '55

St. Brigid of Ireland

BY ALICE CURTAYNE

SHEED AND WARD · NEW YORK · 1954

Nihil Obstat

> *Thomas J. McHugh, LL.D.*
> Censor Librorum

Imprimatur

> ✠ *Henry T. Klonowski, D.D.*
> Administrator, Diocese of Scranton

Date:

> *Scranton, July 6, 1954*

Contents

Contents

St. Brigid of Ireland

ONE

The Women of 450

St. Brigid, who ranks with Patrick and Colum-cille in Ireland's Great Triad of Saints, arose in that period where certainty begins in our record. She stands in that first shaft of light that illuminates our history, literature, topography, art and architecture. The strength of Irish devotion to her is expressed in the very repetition of our Kilbrides, Templebreedys, Tobarbrides, Kilbreedys, Rathbrides and Drumbrides. No one having the slightest acquaintance with Ireland can miss her name, so hugely is it scrawled across the landscape. The ancients affixed it to enduring things, like running water and glens, that should witness to her forever. Both the Liffey and the Lee have tributaries named after her. There is a Bride's Glen near Cabinteely, county Dublin; countless wells and streams, with the characteristic ash tree mirrored in the water, recall her name. Her contemporaries re-named the landmarks, recast the whole topography of the island, in order that she should be remembered.

Her cult is distinguished too, by a certain freshness of enthusiasm. There is still preserved in its texture an element of surprise, a delight, such as men might experience on beholding dawn for the first time. Even after fifteen hundred years her name has never sunk into somnolence, but still vibrates in the ear of the Irish people like a trumpet blast. All this is universally known, but not in the least understood. It is not understood because with the passage of time we have lost sight of the strange singularity of Brigid.

It would not be an exaggeration to say that her appearance was like a new revelation of Christianity. At any rate, as interpreted by her, men in this country had not yet dreamed of its application. Rightly to understand, however, what that Brigidine daybreak portended, one must plunge into the night preceding it. A mental effort must be made to blot out the intervening fifteen centuries of change, so as to live again in the past. Obliterate the present before you begin this story.

Imagine a world in which the idea of—I do not say a career—but any kind of existence for women apart from home life had never been even formulated. One area circumscribed the world of women in Brigid's day: house-keeping. Beyond that horizon lay the unknown world of men's affairs into which women generally had no entrance. All women were absorbed in domestic life, and were never considered in any other connection before the coming of St. Patrick.

Notice, however, that no lugubrious picture of oppression and degradation has to be drawn here. There were many respects in which the women of early Christian Ireland were more emancipated than the women of today. This was especially stressed in all regulations governing marriage. A prospective husband in those days had to pay a dowry to the bride's father—a reversal of modern practice—giving rise to the remark that Ireland was the only place where the wife, rather than the husband, was purchased. After marriage a wife was allowed separate ownership of property, and in all respects her position was practically equal to that of her husband. Cases of ill-treatment or cruelty on the part of the latter were rare, so easy was it for a wife to obtain legal separation. It was even too easy: this constituted one of the difficulties encountered by St. Patrick in pagan Ireland. The Brehon Code laid down seven legitimate reasons for conjugal separation, and probably not half of them would be considered operative in a divorce court today.

Daughters had right of inheritance in Ireland centuries before it was conceded in other countries, and the same liberal tendency is everywhere evident in our ancient literature. The women of 450 had special places or sections in the public assemblies. They had organized games of their own at fairs, and even enclosures reserved for them.

Recall, too, that family life in that era of home-crafts was far more varied and interesting than in our age of syndicated industries. Handwork of all kinds was highly prized. A woman aimed at not merely expertness in feminine employments, but at possessing the implements necessary for them, such as a loom, distaff, spindles, handmill, sieve.

When she owned these, she had increased status, being recognized "a great worker," as it was termed. This status considerably enhanced her matrimonial prospects. In the Ireland of Brigid's day there is no evidence of subjection or injustice in the normal grade of women.

I say "normal," for there was a second class, bond-maidens, or slave-girls, who were far less fortunate. They had no rights. They were frequently grossly treated. Ancient Irish literature is full of anecdotes illustrating the miseries of their position, and Adamnan's Law in particular recounts the injustices they suffered. Chris-

tianity, when they accepted it, became a huge
complexity, for they were not expected or en-
couraged by their masters to live in accordance
with a high moral code. Slave-girls were the
property, body and soul, of their owners. St.
Patrick, in his deep experimental knowledge
of their lives, pitied them profoundly. The fact
that he makes special mention of them in his so
brief *Confession* shows how much their plight
was on his mind:

> Women who are kept in slavery suffer espe-
> cially; they constantly endure even unto ter-
> rors and threats. But the Lord gave grace to
> many of His hand-maidens, for although they
> are forbidden, they earnestly follow the ex-
> ample set them.

Christianity was forbidden to slaves because
it was an inconvenience to slave-owners when
bond-people asserted a right to respect family
ties. All that painful atmosphere of Uncle
Tom's Cabin surrounded the slave question in
Ireland too. A family in bondage rarely escaped
dispersion. A husband might be taken from his
wife and sold at his owner's pleasure to the most
distant purchaser; consorts thus torn apart
would be forcibly provided with other partners;
children in infancy would be taken from their
parents and brought up without any knowledge

of them. When in compliance with Christian laws, resistance was offered to such arbitrary measures, "suffering, terrors and threats" were the portion of slaves.

The work relegated to bondwomen was always of the most monotonous and menial description: swine-herding, grinding corn, washing the feet of guests, holding lights during the entertainment of company. The corn was ground for the most part in rude handmills, or querns, many ancient specimens of which may still be examined in our museums. Though water-mills were employed too, they were not yet in general or frequent use. The method of using the handmill was to pour the grain through a hole in the upper stone of the quern, which was usually turned by two women seated on the ground facing each other. The quern was revolved by rapidly passing from one to the other the handle in the upper stone. This was excessively slow and laborious toil in large households, where bondwomen were sometimes obliged to spend the best part of their day at it. As a detail two women would take an hour to grind only ten pounds of meal. The tedium of holding lights can be readily imagined. It was the practice for one or more bondwomen to stand holding lights by the table while their master supped; and often they were obliged to stand thus for the whole evening until the family retired.

The stage is roughly set for St. Brigid's appearance: a dark stage on which benighted figures flit confusedly. What is remarkable about Brigid is that she did not belong to the women of 450. She stood isolated, without prototype, without peer. When she arose it was as though with a decisive movement she pulled back a heavy curtain shrouding the scene. And at that gesture all the other actors on the stage stand transfigured before a landscape where they see for the first time such freedom as they had never dreamed of, and beyond, Vision, the world opened to them by the Faith.

TWO

The Shaking Sod

THE term used by the old chroniclers in describing periods when domestic wars were prevalent in Ireland was particularly applicable to the seventy years or so of St. Brigid's life. A first glance at this period shows the land convulsed, as though helplessly and irremediably, by internal conflict. One would imagine that poisonous stimulations to strife were exuding from the very soil. Peering across the gulf of fifteen centuries, the modern reader is at first bewildered by the incessant discord. The patiently strenuous efforts of early Christianity could not avail to heal, except very slowly, the rankling feuds.

Recall, however, that to speak of those domestic wars as "civil" would be a misnomer in relation to the period. The structure of society must be borne in mind to understand how con-

tention between the small kingdoms of Ireland
was necessarily as much a commonplace of
daily life as, say, international rivalries and
balance of power questions are in the Europe of
today. Anciently a pentarchy, the "five-fifths of
Ireland" had been replaced in St. Brigid's time
by a heptarchy: the kingdoms of Ailech, Air-
gialla and Ulaid in the north (corresponding
roughly to the area of modern Ulster); Connacht; then Mide and Laigin (approximating
to modern Leinster); and Mumu (corresponding
more or less to the present Munster).

Each of these seven kingdoms was further
subdivided into a number of lesser kingdoms,
or states, that correspond roughly to the present
baronies, and were ruled over by sub-kings.
The sub-kings owed tribute and war service to
their overlords, the seven kings of the heptarchy,
who in turn were immediately subject to the
High King of Ireland, who was, theoretically,
the supreme authority in the land. There were
rivalries, confederacies, and coalitions constantly arising, shifting, disappearing, among
the seven kingdoms, which were, in their turn,
sometimes divided internally by domestic feuds.

In the fifth century Tara was the sole symbol
of the political unity of Ireland. Although the
High King's supremacy was constantly defied,
his office was an institution upholding central

rule, checking to some degree the arrogance of
the seven kings, and tending to unify the states.
All through Brigid's lifetime, Tara upheld the
validity of its sanctions. The triennial assemblies
summoned to the royal residence were a bond
holding the heptarchy together. At the great
Feis of Tara, a "truce of God" used to be proclaimed and homicide there was prohibited so
strictly that death was its penalty. The royal
residence was the focus of the heptarchy—peo-
pled, full of animation, the laughter of ladies
sounding from its grianán, and the mead cir-
cling in its banquet-halls.

The domestic dissensions in fifth-century Ireland are like a tangled skein. But however
roughly and rudely blocked in, it will be found
that the historical background adds enormously
to the understanding of St. Brigid. What is of
peculiar interest is that she was born of the most
belligerent of the kingdoms, and the contention
was closest in that area of Ireland where she
mainly worked. One descries her serene figure
of peace as though in the calm-centre of the
cyclone.

But before entering deeper into contemporary history, a word of caution should be
interpolated. If this account of disruption and
conflict conveys an impression that all sense of
unity, of oneness of race and land, was absent
from the mind of fifth-century Ireland, such

an impression is false. Although power was so decentralized in practice and so disputed, the idea of Ireland as one nation made up of diverse states was clearly formed in the mind of our people long before the most ancient records came into being, since these already contain the idea in a form almost modern in its maturity. In the most ancient of our legends, the land of Erin is already personified as queen reigning over the men of Ireland. If the fifth-century Gaels, therefore, did not think of Ireland as one, in the sense of a political entity, their consciousness of unity and distinctiveness in the deeper sense of nationhood was well developed.

Remember, too, how far ruder and more primitive was the condition of affairs among contemporary peoples, such as the Anglo-Saxons, the Franks, or the Goths, in so far as that condition of affairs can be discerned, or even surmised, for their record begins much later. The fact is that this fifth-century heptarchy marks such a stage of progress that the only near parallel to it is provided by the medieval states of Italy, those free communes that arose one thousand years later. In both groups their very turbulence stands as a symbol of their freedom. They had power of choice.

Returning to the unrest that characterized fifth-century Ireland, three main causes of strife are distinguished. The first and the most im-

portant was the struggle of the Leinstermen
to recover from the Southern Ui Neill possession
of such midland country as had belonged to
Leinster under the pentarchy. This contest
should be remembered as the shifting background to Brigid's activities, if we are to vis-
ualize the contrast between her personality and
her age. No less than fifteen battles are listed in
the Annals between the years 452 and 517, that
is, during her lifetime. All these engagements
were fought in, or on the border of, the midland territory that was in dispute. In the latter
year the Ui Neill won at Druim Derge such a
decisive engagement as forced the Leinstermen
to relinquish their claim to the conquered land
of Meath.

The second source of strife was division
among the Ui Neill family group for possession
of the High King's throne. Every Irish reader
knows something about the High King Laoghaire, through his encounter with St. Patrick.
When this Laoghaire of invidious fame died,
his son Luguid was only a child. Ailill Molt
(whose father had been High King before
Laoghaire) stepped on to the vacant throne. But
when Luguid came of age he effected a sort of
revolution and defeated Ailill Molt at the battle
of Ocha, in 483. For this engagement there was
a formidable muster of the Northern and

Southern branches of the Ui Neill against their kinsfolk from Connacht. Ailill Molt was slain, and Luguid succeeded to the sovereignty of Ireland. St. Brigid, by this year, had reached mature age, the early thirties. The date marks an epoch in Irish history. Luguid's victory wrested the High Kingship of Ireland from the Connacht dynasty and secured it exclusively to the Ui Neill family from that day until the eleventh century.

A third source of contention was Tuathal's bloody legacy to the people, the tribute called the Boramha. Originally levied on Leinster to avenge an insult to the High King's daughters (according to one account), this imposition was unjust in its severity and permanence. Every second year the men of Leinster were condemned to furnish the High King with an enormous booty of kine, hogs, wethers, mantles, silver and cauldrons. Within a few decades of the imposition, Leinster was exasperated and the tribute had to be exacted at the point of the sword. In the tract on the Boramha, forty-one battles are listed as having been fought by the Leinstermen against the High King during the fifty years after the battle of Ocha, almost an average of a battle a year, because of the accursed tax. Laoghaire, St. Patrick's acquaintance, when taken prisoner by the Leinstermen, had sworn by the sun and the wind that he would never again exact the tribute. But on his release he violated his oath, once more invaded Leinster, intent on plundering, and was fittingly—so his enemies believed—killed by the elements.

Besides those three principal knots of strife, there fermented in the Ireland of Brigid's day a weltering criss-cross of minor conflicts. Warfare predominated. In striving to evoke the atmosphere of the fifth century, the reader must hear the clash of arms as the perpetual undertone to all other sounds.

St. Patrick's *Confession* corroborates, for into that calm and humble record of a soul—a record not even remotely concerned with exterior affairs—some rumours of the century's unrest have penetrated. It is evident that the great missionary had to pay heavy sums for his safe-conduct through the contending states and that his work was often carried on at his peril.

> On occasion, I used to give presents to the kings, besides the hire that I gave to their sons who accompany me; and nevertheless they seized me with my companions, and on that day they most eagerly desired to kill me; but my time had not yet come. And everything they found with us they plundered, and me myself they bound with irons. And on the fourteenth day the Lord delivered me from

their power . . . moreover, ye know by proof how much I paid to those who were judges throughout all the districts which I more frequently visited; for I reckon that I distributed to them not less than the price of fifteen men, so that ye might enjoy me. . . . Daily, I expect either slaughter, or to be defrauded, or reduced to slavery, or an unfair attack of some kind.

Picturesque and dramatic was the ancient's mode of conveying the sorrow occasioned by this pressure of domestic contention. There was a legendary belief that when a champion was hard-pressed and imperilled in battle, the shield with which he parried the spear-thrusts roared in protest at his impending fate. That protest resounded all over Ireland, making known who was in peril. Then the shields of all the other champions in the land took up the mourning cry in unison. It re-echoed over the mountains, was prolonged in the bays and along by the rocky coasts. It was heard on sea and the Three Waves of Erin responded: the great wave in Glandore Harbour in Cork roared its solemn awareness; the great wave beyond the mouth of the Bann in Derry boomed an answer; and the great wave in Dundrum Bay, off the County Down, clamoured with its deep cry. Grandiose concept that this triangle of roaring, surging water should make the lament for an island disaster and prolong it indefinitely far out over the great wastes of the sea.

In this war-riven land Brigid was born, as has been said, of the kingdom that was the most persistently belligerent, Leinster of the battles. Her birth-place was Faughart, three miles from Dundalk, in the County Louth, and the date was about the year 453. Her father was Dubthach (pronounced Duffack, its modern equivalent being Duffy), a pagan petty king or chieftain, and her mother was a Christian bondwoman named Brocessa, who belonged to his household.

This is the account given in three of the six "Lives" contained in Colgan's *Triadis Thaumaturgae*, one of the three hagiographers being Bishop Ultan. The other three "Lives" are vague on the matter of parentage. Now, while it is impossible to imagine anyone who was devoted to St. Brigid, as all these writers were, setting down such an account if it were not true, or setting it down as mere hearsay without verifying it, on the other hand one can readily comprehend a preference to be silent on the matter.

Before the birth of Brigid, Dubthach's wife forced him to sell Brocessa to a distant buyer, a Druid who lived westwards, in what then seemed the faraway kingdom of Connacht. As was customary in such transactions, the offspring was reserved to the original owner, which means that when Brigid reached the age to be useful, she was claimed back into Dubthach's household and assumed her mother's rôle there, grinding the quern, washing the feet of guests, tending the sheep on the mountain, or herding the animals of the farm.

Tradition and pious hagiographers have combined to burnish the story with the usual circumstances of a saint's birth: inspired prophecies, both by pagan and Christian authorities, told the future greatness of this child, upon whom the world smiled not; splendid and terrific auguries from heaven indicated that she who appeared to be among the least was in reality first. Brocessa had no rights, no court of appeal, no defender, she could not even keep her child. But over the hut where the bondmaid slept "a flame and a fiery pillar" were seen. Three clerics in white shining vestments, such as might attend for the christening of a queen's child, came to baptize the babe, giving her a name. They were said to be angels. There was no drapery for Brigid's cradle, but a curtain of flame hung softly over it. Later, when the child was left sleeping in the stable where the mother was working, the very cowdung seemed to ignite suddenly like a prairie fire, and when the servants ran to it they found no heat in that sudden blaze, only light.

If the account of St. Brigid's parentage be exact, she derived one advantage from it: that complete disregard for the accident of birth nearly always expressed by the children of unequal unions. As we shall see, it was her habit in later life to converse with kings as with equals and to treat slave-girls as sisters, whose freedom she passionately claimed. Before leaving the circumstances of her birth, it may be well to warn the reader against misinterpreting them by reading the twentieth century into the fifth. In a country still largely pagan, the public attitude to such matters was fundamentally different from that of our time. Furthermore, apart altogether from the Christian view-point, a man's status was by no means rendered so inseparable from his birth as it is now. In the ancient Irish polity the ruling principle was "that a man is better than his birth." Even a slave, could he secure his manumission, would find the world open to him. He could improve his status indefinitely and with comparative ease by the purchase of land, by personal economies, work, the exercise of talent, or by learning.

But Brigid had not a happy childhood. The new slave girl, conducted from Connacht to Dubthach's household in Leinster, carried out submissively the daily routine of her kind, but

was capable too of sudden disconcerting ges-
tures, like those of a princess. When a beggar
asked for an alms from this shepherd girl, who
in all other respects was the soul of discretion,
she might, likely as not, hand him with regal
munificence a sheep from her flock. Especially
it was observed that numbers and quantities
seemed to play the oddest tricks with her. Once,
for instance, five guests arrived, and she was
given five pieces of bacon to cook for them.
This time it was a hungry dog who licked her
hand and whined imploringly. Brigid could not
resist him. She gave him a piece. Someone com-
plained of her, and as wrath was breaking out
the five pieces were found in the pot. All the
traditional stories of Brigid's girlhood are on
the same theme: her bounty, and the intervention of supernatural agencies to avert drastic
punishment. The stories ring true, because for
the most part they are at once extraordinary
and trivial. If a later biographer were minded
to invent miracles for Brigid, he would use
rather more imagination and tell of something
more impressive than a little food conveyed
furtively to a dog.

But there was one in that household whom
no flashing of minor miracles could appease,
Dubthach's wife, who was not pleased. In the
end, to promote the peace of his household,
Dubthach was obliged to send Brigid away, as

he had similarly disposed of Brocessa. This resolve led to one of the most dramatic episodes of Brigid's early life.

Dubthach summoned her one morning from drudgery and placed her in his chariot. As they drove off their conversation was as elliptical as those dialogues in the Gospel narrative. We are told in the oldest "Life" of Brigid that the father said roughly: "It is not to honour you I am taking you." Clearly the girl, innocently delighted with her drive, must have been beaming at the surly chieftain. And he added: "I am taking you to sell you: it will be the king's quern now you will have to grind." The monarch in question was the King of Leinster, her father's overlord, reputed to have been baptized by St. Patrick. No answer is reported from the child, whose joy was so suddenly dashed out. Arriving at the king's fortress, her father went in to strike a bargain, to haggle mayhap about the price of Brigid's service. Meanwhile he left her waiting in the chariot. As it happened, he had placed his sword near her on the seat. Then a leper appeared at the side of the vehicle and begged her for alms.

There is much in the record of our early history perplexing to the modern Christian reader. For example, all the purely pagan elements seem to us who are formed out of Christianity almost like the account of another race. Yet there are many other factors in the life of Celtic Ireland inducing the Christian to feel instantly at home. One such point of contact is the treatment of lepers.

In ancient Jewry, lepers were shrouded, isolated, and provided with bells to warn the world of their approach. The clean had time to flee. Men made no effort to repress the sentiments of loathing inspired by lepers, who were outcast. But in Celtic Ireland, even before its evangelization, these sufferers were, on account of their misfortune, privileged members of the community. And as a result they often became obstreperous and impudent to a degree. In fifth-century Ireland leprosy seems to have been the incurable scourge, as cancer is today. But unlike their Jewish forerunners, the Irish lepers went about freely, were compassionately tolerated, received bountiful alms and liberal medical help. This indulgence was not, perhaps, hygienic, but it was exceedingly humane.

When that dreadful deformity first appeared near Brigid, the mournful eyes looking at her out of a ravaged face above a ruined tower of manhood, her heart, already heavy with apprehension, sank, for she had nothing to give. The leper was asking in God's name for charity. Looking desperately around, her eye caught the flash of jewels in the hilt of her father's sword on the seat. She lifted the heavy weapon and gave it to the mendicant, who quickly made off.

As a symbol, the meaning of this scene can never be exhausted. I can merely hint at its meaning. It is one of the many great scenes that tell pictorially the Christian story, that sum up the Gospel: like the scene of Patrick's fire on Slane, or Columcille dying before the altar at Iona, or St. Elizabeth of Hungary showing her husband an apronful of flowers, or St. Francis of Assisi, seven centuries later, springing from his horse to embrace just such another afflicted wretch.

Brigid's behaviour is not easy to understand. She was in disgrace. She was about to be punished precisely for actions of that kind: a habit of the wildest bounty. She was just then filled with dread of the unknown, of an authority higher than her father's intervening to bring her to order. At that moment, within the fortress, the King of Leinster, not without surprise, was asking Dubthach why he wanted to sell the girl, and the chieftain was explaining that he could not keep her, because of her open-handedness to the poor, that nothing was safe in her keeping, that his wife compelled him for this reason to get rid of her. The king asked to see her and Dubthach returned to his chariot to call Brigid. Instantly he missed the sword, prized above all his possessions, that blade of whose temper and reliability he was so proud, that had served him well in many an engagement, and we are told by the old "Life" that he was "mightily enraged." Indeed, the harassed father must have asked himself whether he was dealing with complete vacuity of mind, or with malignant perversity. To all this furious raving about the value of the weapon, Brigid insisted doggedly that that was why she had given it to God.

She was taken before the king, and as he was a Christian, he came nearer to understanding her. Perhaps some flash of premonition disturbed him. He was a man who still, of necessity, depended mainly on his sword for the enforcement of justice and the maintenance of his kingdom. Yet he must have sensed, however dimly, that in this scene outside his fortress gate a girl—a mere slave-girl at that—had lifted up the sword of the spirit against the sword of might, had spoken a challenge, had joined issue in some contest of magnitude and importance, had opened an epoch. And Dubthach's bad day reached its climax when he heard his king saying to him: "Leave her alone, for her merit before God is greater than ours." Brigid was taken back home.

One of our ancient legends tells of a sword presented to a champion by the queen of some fairy mansion: a sword so marvellous that when raised it shot out in length and filled the heavens like the curve of a rainbow. But when Brigid handed away her warrior father's sword, as though it were a thing of no account, there occurred a far greater marvel. For she flung out a banner that is streaming still after fifteen centuries. In that moment she began to marshal an army, in whose ranks unnumbered hosts of the women of Ireland were to march—and are marching today—in peaceful conquest of the world. This strange creature, in whose veins flowed the blood of Conn of the Hundred Battles, is represented as making an entirely new proclamation to an age absorbed in war, and the terms were to appeal forever to Irish hearts. She lifted up for all a nobler aspiration, not to be fulfilled by the sword; a judgment not to be effected by the sword; and a cause, the greatest of all causes, which the sword is not called upon to serve.

And if this episode be legend merely, its interest and value are still compelling. It is valuable in the way all tradition is valuable, it enshrines a character. The first public gesture recorded of this daughter of a Leinster sub-king is her rejection of the sword. In relation to her disturbed age this suggests an early independence of mind and character that is in perfect accord with all our other knowledge of Brigid.

THREE

The Fiery Arrow

A PICTURE of the next phase of Brigid's progress is presented in a few lines of the Irish "Life" preserved in the *Leabhar Breac*:—

> On a time it came into Brigid's mind, through the grace of the Holy Ghost, to go and see her mother, who was in bondage. So she asked her father's leave, and he gave it not. Nevertheless she went without Dubthach's permission. Her mother was toil-worn and sickly. She was glad when Brigid arrived. Brigid tended her and set about putting the dairy to rights.

The majority of the "Lives" conclude the account of the sword episode by saying that in this way Brigid was delivered from bondage. In the Ireland of her day the redeeming of slaves was held to be an act of mercy. Whether Dubthach felt obliged to give his daughter freedom on the king's recommendation, or whether he was prompted by a wish for household peace, or by his own tardy generosity, we shall never know. It is probable that when he failed to place her in a suitable household, the alternative of disposing of her in marriage immediately occurred to him. Worldly shrewdness would have prompted him to aim at an alliance advantageous to himself, and the first step in this plan was to give her her rightful status. It is clear anyhow that through the sword episode Brigid was released from bondage and that thenceforward she was not merely free, but considered herself entitled even to disregard her father's wishes, when these appeared unreasonable to her Christian mind.

Already in her girlhood the lines of an exceptionally strong character are emerging. Her freedom won, the first use she made of it was to succour her mother, whose health was poor, but who was still engaged in the heavy labours of quern and churn. Brigid went to her, and by the simple expedient of personally undertaking the work, enabled her mother to rest. But first, how did Brigid, alone, and under the ban of her father's displeasure, accomplish the arduous journey to her mother? So far as one can piece the story together, it involved traversing the whole breadth of Ireland. In this case one can only regret that the meagreness of the primary sources prevents us from accompanying Brigid in her journey.

She found her mother in charge of a mountain dairy herd of twelve cows. Brocessa had to do the milking morning and evening and set the milk in pans for the cream to rise. This was skimmed off and put aside for butter-making, while the skim milk was fed to calves. The entire work connected with twelve cows so managed would be considered heavy for a modern land-girl. Brigid cheerfully undertook it and was thus happily engaged for some time when trouble arose.

Here, just as on her father's farm, she found the poor irresistible. When they appeared at the dairy door in obvious need, she gave them not only skim milk, but butter, too. One beggar always brought others on the following day. Soon the other farm workers were murmuring about Brigid's generosity with their master's goods, and some rumour of the argument reached his ear. He sent for the herd to question him. The next line of the anecdote gives us another glimpse of Brigid's powerful personality at an early age, since we are told that the herd "dared not speak ill of her in her absence." He gave evasive answers that naturally annoyed his master, who was then left with no option but to go to the dairy himself and see what was going

on. Master and mistress together paid it a surprise visit, taking with them a huge hamper in
which to collect the stores of butter that should
be there. Just as at the present day, that weight
of butter could be calculated to a nicety, according to the season of the year.

They found Brigid singing at her work, surrounded by bowls of milk and firkins of butter.
She appears to have been a particularly efficient
dairymaid, and this is not the only time she
will be seen in such surroundings. In her role
of bondwoman, she now began by washing her
visitors' feet and serving them food. But they
did not see on the shelves sufficient butter even
to half fill their hamper. Brigid, however, began
composedly to lay in her supply. She filled and
filled, and the yellow butter seemed ever between her hands, though where it came from the
onlookers could not see. Believing they were in
the presence of the supernatural, and remembering, too, the auguries of her birth and childhood,
this kindly master and his wife at once conferred
on Brigid the cows and all the produce of that
mountain dairy. But the girl pleaded an alternative gift, her mother's freedom, urging her
age, her ill-health, her present unfitness for toil.
This wish was granted, and it seems that with
the help of the master, who afterwards became
a Christian, Brigid was able to see her mother

installed in permanent security and peace. She then returned to her father.

Dubthach now made one final effort to order his daughter's life in the way he believed it should go. As is the practice even today among worthy Irish fathers, he arranged a marriage for her. Since he had raised her to the status of freedom, he naturally thought he might as well make the best of her by strengthening his own position through a suitable alliance. If the enquiry be not irreverent, let us look for a moment at this extraordinary girl's qualifications for matrimony. Her personal appearance enters into the question. She must have been very strong, for her skill in farmwork was famous. Indeed, Brigid's whole life is remarkably different from most saints' lives in this: that illness, disease, or physical suffering played no part in it.

All the oldest "Lives" and traditions lay stress on the fact that she was beautiful. We know from her manner of life that she must have had that bloom and grace which are acquired only in the open air, and with which Nature rewards those who keep her company. There are counterparts of Brigid in Ireland yet. If you meet the type, look at it, for it is something that tends to disappear from the earth. I have seen it but a few times in my life along the lonely roads of the Kerry *Gaelthacht.* A girl, perhaps driving home the cows in the evening, barefoot, dressed in such nondescript garments one is uncertain what they comprise—an old coat, a frock—or whether their colour be black or brown; garments anyhow that never were fashionable and that have served for seasons beyond memory. Yet, instead of having to dress in order to acquire distinction, this girl wears her dun garb with such regal grace as actually to confer splendour upon it. She carries out her task thoughtfully, self-possessedly, humbly, but with a carriage that is to be envied, not imitated; with a poise not seen in city drawingrooms; with one of those faces, at once brilliant and still, that appear to reflect the very light of day, in which all tranquillity seems to end. Brigid must have looked like this girl.

Of her suitor only two details are supplied, the most meagre details, hardly sufficient for the construction of a personage: that he was a man of chaste life and a poet. Here I am bound to digress, because I know what the modern reader is thinking and I must disabuse his mind. Reading the twentieth century into the fifth, he will concede that these qualities are wholly admirable of course but—inadequate. He will jump to the crude conclusion that a poet in the Ireland of Brigid's day was in the unfortunate position of a poet in our day. He will call to mind some poetic but penurious friend of his: an amiable personage, with the sweet, apologetic manner of the unsuccessful literary craftsman; one universally liked but universally commiserated; always applauded but never taken seriously. And he will end his false parallel by believing that even from the most mundane point of view Dubthach's daughter would have been right in rejecting this offer.

It was not so. In Celtic Ireland the muse was exalted. The poet was highly, even excessively, remunerated for his services to the community. He was not then down-at-heel. He wore rich apparel; he dined well; he drank deep; he swaggered. He had property and servants. He travelled about with a retinue and his whole life was passed in visits and entertainment. At table he had to have the seat of honour and the choicest cut from the joint.

He ranked next the king and had real power. Intense discomfort was always experienced by the offender who incurred the poet's displeasure. Noblemen fawned on him because they dreaded his satire far more than advancing enemy cohorts bristling with spears. No one dared refuse to a poet even the most preposterous request. He was often, as an individual, spoiled and arrogant.

Let it be understood, however, that no mere

poetaster could attain this position: the poet had to pass through a twelve years' course, from which he emerged with considerably more than a knowledge of versification. He was a man of learning and a philosopher, one of the three members of society entitled by law to speak in public (the druid and the brehon, or judge, were the other two). Dubthach, then, in desiring a poet for son-in-law, showed that he was shrewd and longheaded. He was also offering Brigid the highest social position.

She refused. She rejected not only this marriage, but all idea of marriage for herself. The authentic Brigid touch comes out in the conclusion of this episode. She did not wish to see her suitor discomfited and she endeavoured to console him. She told him what to do in order to find a good wife and promised him her blessing on "his face and his speech" when the critical moment came to ask for the lady's hand.

Despite the expostulations and even the jeers of the members of her family, she persevered in her intention to become what the ancient Irish called "a virgin of Christ." She proceeded to play a part, small at first, in that great movement towards monasticism which St. Patrick found so astonishing in his Irish converts. The apostle wrote in his *Confession*:

See how in Ireland there has lately been
formed a people of the Lord. . . . Sons and
daughters of Irish chieftains are seen to become monks and nuns . . . and their number
increases more and more.

And we have already seen how his special
sympathy went out to bondwomen who strove
so valiantly to lead the Christian life in defiance
of pagan masters.

Brigid was one of those pioneers who evoked
Patrick's admiration and sympathy. But the re-
vised chronology of his life disposes of the belief
that she was a co-worker with the Apostle. If
St. Patrick died in the year 461, and if Brigid
was born in 453, then she can have been only
a child of eight when the Apostle died.

The first fifth-century Irish nuns apparently
continued to live in their own homes after they
had consecrated their lives to God. They divided up their days as best they could between
service to the mission, corporal works of mercy,
and prayer. Their service to the mission chiefly
took the form of needlework: they made vestments, altar cloths, and tapestries for the adorn-
ment of the newly-built churches. But whether
their vocation was secure or threatened depended not on their own will but absolutely
on family circumstances. Apart from actual
interference, their lot was hard. In their isola-

tion they suffered from lack of that support imparted in community life. But often, too, they were persecuted by their families. Even St. Patrick marvelled at their constancy. "They do it," he tells us, "not with the consent of their fathers; but they endure persecution and lying reproaches from their kindred."

It was Brigid who changed the face of things and saved the early Irish feminine ascetic movement. She saved it by the innovation of community life. From the moment her mother's liberty was ensured and her father's objections silenced, she began the organization of women. She had seven companions with her when she went to be received into the religious life. Those eight seem never again to have separated.

The friend whom she sought for this historic ceremony was Bishop Mel, whose church was on Croghan Hill in Offaly. He was absent when Brigid and her companions arrived, but they followed him to Fartullagh in Westmeath, where he received them. This was the origin of Brigid's close connection with the Ardagh diocese. She was soon to found a community at Croghan Hill and another in Westmeath.

The old "Lives" speak of the nun, Brigid, as dressed in white: *"pallium album et vestem candidam,"* almost the same description being repeated in her Breviary office. This idea of her appearance is disturbed by the fact that a church in Bruges possesses a circular cloak, said to be hers, and the colour of this cloak is red, but not a defiant, undoubted red, since her most recent biographer describes the colour as "dyed with Tyrian blue." A portion of this mantle is in the possession of the Redemptoristine nuns, Drumcondra, and it is described as purple-red. There are three paintings of St. Brigid by Irish artists, and it is interesting to see how they have decided this point: Patrick Tuohy shows her dressed in red; Leo Whelan shows her dressed in white; and Gabrielle Hayes, the most recent Irish artist to attempt this subject, shows her in a white dress with a red cloak.

Brigid did not live an enclosed life. In her case going into a convent meant becoming one of the most indefatigable travellers in the land. She is one of the most interesting products of Irish monasticism. This movement, throughout the sixth century, invariably expressed itself in the most strenuous apostolic work for souls, rather than in retirement and contemplation. But the emphasis was dictated by emergency rather than by choice. Celtic Christianity held that the anchoretical life was the highest possible to man, but the monk's desire for the desert was, in a manner, frustrated by his love for his brethren's spiritual welfare. This struggle between an ideal and a mode of life—typical of Irish monasticism—is well exemplified in the life of Brigid.

All who have suffered persecution instinctively succour the persecuted. Brigid's experience of the relief of community life sent her out at once, offering the same security to all the women in the land who shared her aspirations. Paradoxically, it is the nun in the freedom of her own home who is like a bird in a cage. To her the difference between the family and a religious community is the difference between imprisonment and liberty, even between death and life.

Thus Brigid's mission began to emerge inevitably. She had personally tested that the Church in Ireland was already strong enough to protect communities of women. Her work, then, was to rescue the nuns of Ireland from the fortresses of chieftains and the hovels of bondwomen, offering them a haven. They needed but a leader to summon them out and she sprang to their guiding.

The poetical derivation of her name is Fiery Arrow. It may be taken as a symbol of her singular independence of mind, which finds no explanation in her epoch or in her circumstances. It expresses, too, the sudden and spirited swiftness with which she assumed and centralized control of a situation teeming with difficulties. It was as though she sent up a signal, like a rocket that summons a muster. The women of the Seven Kingdoms looked up from their sunbowers, from their querns, or their looms, they looked up from the darkness of their discouragement. And so unerring was Brigid's guidance, so winged with resolve, so touched with divine fire, they gave her an instant and ardent response.

FOUR

Brigid and the Bishops

THE bishops of Ireland extended their friendship to Brigid, and this later developed into a kind of fellowship with the episcopacy—one of the most curious features of her life. Ten or twelve years before her birth, St. Patrick had already established the Irish hierarchy under the primacy of Armagh. The courtesy title of bishop was frequently given in the early Irish Church to abbots, or heads of monastic foundations, who exercised jurisdiction in the surrounding territory. Anyhow, all the foremost ecclesiastical figures of her day appear to have immediately discerned Brigid's merit and to have received her unhesitatingly on terms of equality. There is no hint in her career of difficulties with church authority, which is such a sorrowful commonplace in the lives of later saints.

The church in which St. Brigid originally

sought to be received is situated high up on the slope of Croghan Hill. Down to the present day she is particularly venerated in all that part of Offaly.

The portents of her greatness, so eloquent at her birth, were renewed at her reception into religion. A column of fire descended over her head and was seen by the assistants in the church. She rested her hand for an instant on the edge of the wooden altar, and at once all that part of the dry seasoned timber became green. This poetic episode would serve as an illustration for the Mass Offertory which says: "Wood hath hope; if it be cut, it groweth green again, and the boughs thereof sprout." What a portent of hope for Ireland was this young girl taking the veil—a symbol of hope that in her land the Church, the Mass, the Altar, would always prevail.

St. Mel, said to have been a nephew of St. Patrick, received her final vows. By this time Brigid's fame was being bruited abroad so insistently that Mel asked her to found a convent for professed nuns under his jurisdiction at Ardagh, and even gave her the site. The first convent at Croghan Hill seems to have been retained as a novitiate. The precise location of Brigid's first community cannot, however, be established with certitude; nor the order of her foundations; nor their number. Let readers remember that the itinerary even of her great model Patrick similarly cannot be written. He himself gives no indication in his *Confession* of the number and sequence of his foundations and admits that he shrinks from the hugeness of such a recital: "It would be a tedious task to explain it all in detail or even in part." Anyhow the whole question of the site of the Brigidine foundations, their sequence and their total, is of academic rather than human interest.

St. Patrick's evangelizing campaign must be recalled in order to understand the method of Brigid, who imitated him with literal faithfulness. "Founding" in the early Christian sense meant something far more strenuous than blessing the first stone. The convents then were, as a rule, clusters of wattle and clay huts, enclosed by great stone or earthen walls. When Brigid founded such a settlement, she had first to supervise the building. Then she had to provide the furnishings and staff the place with a few competent sisters whom she had trained. When she had the machinery in motion, she left them in charge and hastened on with a companion or two to a fresh field.

Like St. Patrick, she had adventures in a chariot. Not organizing ability merely, nor a measure of resolve rare in woman, but physical courage, too, of the highest order was required

for the work to which she had set her hand. The
chariot, which solved all the transport problems
of Celtic Ireland, was drawn usually by two
horses and was a vehicle shaped like the gig still
used in the Irish countryside. It was, perhaps,
lower, more comfortable, and heavier than the
gig. The ancient Irish were famous chariot-
makers and the epic tales contain many descrip-
tions of the chariots of the rich: with ebony
shafts, gold and silver fittings, silk upholstery,
plumes for ornamentation, and sometimes, too,
the woodwork was inlaid with precious stones.
Brigid's car was probably strictly utilitarian.
She became an indefatigable traveller on the
open road, testing her physical endurance to the
utmost by visits that connected up her convents.
She had a driver, who sat on a small seat in
front, while two nuns usually sat with her inside
the vehicle.

Some of those journeys involved immense
distances, often over rough roads, or rivers, and
with mettlesome horses. Brigid and peril became
familiars. There are two different stories of acci-
dents in which she was flung out of the chariot.
The second time this happened, her head struck
a stone and was cut open.

The priest-chaplain of one of her monastic
settlements often acted as driver for the nuns
on their missionary journeys. On one of those
expeditions, the driver began to explain some

point of doctrine to his passengers. He became so interested in his theme that he turned almost right round in his seat, letting the reins lie slack on the backs of the horses. One of them slipped his neck from the head collar and ran free, but so absorbed were the three in their spiritual conversation, they never noticed what had happened until both horses stopped short, of their own accord, at the edge of a precipice.

Another day, when Brigid was being driven by a workman in her employment, he insisted on taking a short cut home by going through a field that was private property and in process of being fenced. The labourers working on the fence objected, and a free fight ensued between them and the driver. Brigid had to get down and separate the combatants before she could proceed.

She crossed the Shannon to establish convents in Roscommon and elsewhere in the west. One of the stories in this connection has a very modern ring. When Brigid was returning home from one of those missions to the west, the boatmen in Athlone asked for exorbitant payment for rowing her and her companions to the opposite shore. The saint was indignant and refused to agree. She then blessed the river and it swiftly sank so low that the little party were able to drive across the river bed.

Although the dates make it impossible to count Patrick among the bishops, abbots, preceptors, counsellors, and friends who helped Brigid in her career, it is at least certain that these included the Apostle's closest friends. She was the intimate friend of churchmen who had been intimate with Patrick; through them she knew his mind. Therefore this statement in the *Book of Armagh* may be taken as essentially true:

> Between St. Patrick and St. Brigid, the columns on which all Ireland rested, a cordial friendship existed, such that they were one in heart and soul.

One such intimate of Patrick's who became a devoted friend of Brigid's was Erc of Slane, that "sweet-voiced Brehon," who was the first to honour Patrick at the court of King Laoghaire. A striking picture of that scene in Tara Hall as Patrick entered is sketched in a few lines of the *Tripartite Life*:

> They were biding before him with the rims of their shields against their chins, and none of them rose up before him save one man only in whom was a nature from God, namely Erc, son of Deg.

An enviable tribute to Erc has come down in record: Patrick's judgment of him, expressed in one sentence—*Everything that he did was just.* Erc afterwards became Bishop of Ardfert, in Kerry, and was tutor to that most astonishing navigator-saint, Brendan of the Voyages, whose name became a European inspiration.

Many of Brigid's chariot journeys were undertaken under Erc's direction. He brought her on a tour of Munster in order personally to direct her in the work of establishing new foundations in his territory. Besides Munster, she travelled all Ireland, and there still remain throughout the whole land legendary traces of her passing.

The importance assumed by Brigid in the eyes of the episcopacy has given rise to at least one absurd legend, which must be dismissed. One reads that Brigid "appointed" Conlaeth to Kildare, almost as though she had conferred episcopal jurisdiction upon him. It is true that Brigid's chief foundation, Kildare, preserved for many centuries a double line of succession of abbesses and of bishops; and it is equally true that for long the nomination of the Bishop of Kildare appeared subject to some extent to the Abbess's approval. This legend is but an illustration of her strong-mindedness, the deference ungrudgingly accorded her by the episcopacy, and the great honour paid in memory of her to her successors at Kildare. She was the admired friend and the counsellor of bishops.

Brigid is credited with an epigrammatic mode

of speech and a certain imperiousness of manner, even with bishops. Once a bishop, with some companions, came to her convent to deliver a sermon. They had come a long journey and greeted her with the news that they were hungry. "So are we hungry—for instruction," she answered. "Go into the church and speak first, and then you shall eat."

Once seven bishops went to visit her, and they have become famous as the Seven Bishops of Cabinteely. Do you suppose Brigid was disturbed by that invasion? No. She sent one sister to the cows that had already been milked twice that day, and another sister to a larder that was as empty as Mother Hubbard's; yet another sister to an ale-vat that was drained dry. But the bishops feasted adequately, for food was a commodity Brigid never failed to find her guests.

There is a charming story told of one Bishop Bron who, journeying to Brigid with some companions, lost the way. Finding themselves stranded in a wilderness at nightfall, they had to sleep in the open. Then all were comforted by the same dream. They thought, as they drowsed in chill discomfort, that through the darkness and wild weather they beheld the lights of Brigid's settlement and that, stumbling to it, they saw her come smiling to the gates to lavish upon them the hospitality for which she was famous. First the feet of the footsore guests were washed, and then, installed in repose, warmth, security, they were given good food in that delightful atmosphere of solicitude that was peculiarly Brigid's. So restful was this dream, the pilgrims suffered not in the least from their night's exposure. They were even refreshed, and with daylight they hopefully resumed their trudge. And lo, at a turn of the road, their hearts soared on seeing the familiar figure driving towards them. The Mother Abbess, having been supernaturally warned, had come out to rescue them from their plight.

Brigid's achievements and power, when contrasted with her lack of training, stand out most singularly. In this display of creative genius, plainly she had divine gifts. She was able to combine the roles of Martha and Mary. The bishops did not wait for a decree of canonization to acclaim that which was manifest. But when it was discovered that she possessed, too, a genuine discernment of souls, people began to flock to her from every side. All the great in the land, including the hierarchy, and the humble, too, and pagans as well as Christians, then began to cultivate her acquaintance.

FIVE

Kildare

THE most famous of all Brigid's foundations and the crown of her labours was her Leinster convent at Kildare, or Cill-dara, her Cell of the Oak. It was the reigning King of Leinster who had given her the site, a clay ridge overlooking the great plain of the Liffey. Brigid's own cell of wattle and clay was built in the shelter of a giant oak, favourite and much admired land-mark in the district that flourished in all its beauty until the tenth century.

It is interesting to find the oak tree thus securely planted and much loved right at the opening of our history. The third saint in our Triad, Columcille, was Brigid's rival in praise of the oak. When he went into exile, his home-sickness centred especially on his little grove of oaks that he had left behind in Ireland; it was the memory of these that tore his heart. Everyone knows the place held by the oak in English history, but not everyone knows that the native Irish originally had the very same attitude towards this royal tree. They could even have taught the English how to appreciate it for its beauty and for its multiple uses. Unhappily for Ireland, her oak forests were looted by the invader, and there are sad records of Irish oak being exported to England to make ships for sending more soldiers and exploiters to our land. A nation shorn of its oak trees is, like Samson shorn of his hair, a nation without strength. Not content with plundering the forests, the despoiler then spread abroad the untruth that the Irish could not appreciate trees. The truth is that trees, and especially the oak, so crowd our ancient history, one can hardly see the lines through the foliage. The planting of oaks in Ireland would be a wonderful gesture of veneration of Brigid, whose name is so inseparably entwined with the oak.

Brigid set up in Kildare a great religious centre, modelled on the settlements of St. Patrick, which in turn had been copied, more or less, from the plan of a chieftain's homestead. When I speak of Brigid occupying a clay and wattle cell, it must not be imagined that the nuns shivered in inadequate shelters that were exposed to the elements on a bleak countryside.

In truth no modern village presents such a compact, secure and warm appearance as did a fifth-century conventual settlement.

The present ruins at Kildare give no clue to the plan of Brigid's original settlement there. The Celtic foundation was destroyed by the Danes in the middle of the ninth century. The present structure dates from the thirteenth century. It has had a chequered history. It was almost destroyed in the Irish Rebellion of 1641. It was again re-built and was again left in ruins after the wars of the seventeenth century. The present reconstructed building dates from 1896.

But there are other ruins in the land from which some guidance may be had, because all the larger monastic settlements of the fifth century were of similar design. Of these the only ruins that have been scientifically investigated are the Nendrum Celtic Monastery remains in Island Mahee, County Down. Happily I know this site. Very often, when a converted pagan chieftain donated a settlement to the Church, his gift to the monks was an ancient fortress, already enclosed by those massive drybuilt triple cashels of pre-Christian origin, such as may be traced so clearly in the Nendrum ruins. The outer surrounding wall, or cashel, built of stone, eight or nine feet thick, was furnished with ramparts of sods on top and with heavy wooden gates, perhaps six feet wide. This wall enclosing the settlement was elliptical and was separated from a second surrounding wall by a broad passageway, used as a walk. A third and inner wall was similarly divided from the second by a broad walk. The space thus triply protected was traversed through the centre by an avenue leading up to the main building of the enclosure, the church. This, in the larger monastic settlements, was usually built of wood and roofed with straw. The artisans' dwellings, or artificers' workshops, lined this main pathway. Since these monastic settlements were self-supporting, producing and consuming all the necessaries of life, the staff in the community's service was numerous. Among the little wooden buildings were usually a smithy, carpenter's shop, cornmill, granary, barn, cowhouse, kiln, gamestore, larder, refectory, kitchen, guest chambers and a library, where manuscripts hung in satchels from the walls. Beyond the church were grouped the community cells, snugly roofed with thatch, the earthen floors warmly strewn with rushes.

Such enclosures were usually set in fields that formed part of the community's grant of land, and were farmed for the nuns' support. It will be understood, then, what hives of industry were those settlements, where all varieties of farmwork, tillage, and pasturage were carried on, in addition to shearing, spinning, weaving, dyeing; where frequently, too, there was a school for the instruction of converts; where church vestments were made and embroidered; where travellers had an asylum; where the poor were sure of finding alms, and the afflicted succour. It is not surprising that all the bishops of Ireland soon required Brigid to found a convent in their districts.

A curious story is told in connection with the building of this settlement at Kildare. While Brigid, accompanied by Bishop Mel, was absorbed in tracing its site, there passed across the Curragh a procession of one hundred horses, dragging loads of wattles. This material belonged to a Leinster chieftain named Ailill, who intended to build a new house. But the wattles were precisely what Brigid wanted, especially as they were conveniently pared and peeled for use. She sent one of her sisters to ask Ailill, who was accompanying his convoy, to make her a present of the loads. The indignant chieftain refused with a curt negative. Immediately, as though stricken with paralysis, the hundred horses fell to the ground; no shouting, kicking, goading, or whipping on the part of the drivers could make them budge. The harassed Ailill found he could not get his wattles home unless his men unloaded and carried them, little by little, on their backs. In the end, of course, he left them there to Brigid. And it shows the fundamental good humour of the chieftain that, furthermore, he caused to be erected such buildings as she required, employing the highest skilled labour.

The Kildare foundation rapidly grew to such magnitude that it assumed the proportions of a city, and a bishop had to be appointed to the jurisdiction of the territory. Conlaeth, a recluse, who was famous as a metal-worker before he received Holy Orders, and who subsequently won fame as "Brigid's Brazier," was appointed to the charge. He was renowned as one of the "three chief artisans of Ireland," the other two being Tassach, St. Patrick's craftsman, and Daig, craftsman of Ciaran of Saighir. Conlaeth established in connection with the Kildare convent a monastery of monks, who founded a school of metal-work and penmanship. There is preserved to this day a crozier, said to have belonged to St. Finbarr of Termon-Barry, Connacht, and to have been made by Conlaeth.

There began to pour out over Ireland, from this school at Kildare, quantities of bells, croziers, chalices, patens, bookrests, and shrines to supply the wants of the mission. But Kildare's special product was manuscripts, many of them so gorgeously illuminated that, though they have

perished, their fame persists, imperishable.
There was a *Book of Kildare*, one of the greatest
of our lost treasures. It was examined in the
twelfth century by Giraldus Cambrensis, that
most prejudiced and mendacious of historians,
who travelled through Ireland with one eye shut
and the other half-open, as it were, that he
might see only what was discreditable to the
country he disliked. Yet, he was pleased with
Kildare and particularly with its Book.

> . . . In it there are almost as many different
> figures as there are pages, highly adorned with
> various colours. Here you may see the Face of
> the Divine Majesty, admirably expressed: here
> the mystic symbols of the Evangelists, now with
> six, now with four wings, now with wings
> twain: here the eagle, there the calf; here the
> face of the man, there of the lion; and other
> figures, almost endless. If you look at these
> superficially and in the usual way, with less
> attention, they will seem a blot rather than a
> knot; you would not expect any ingenuity,
> where nevertheless, there is nothing but in-
> genuity. But if you were to apply keenness of
> vision to a closer scrutiny, and concentrate
> much more deeply into the secrets of the art,
> you will be able to observe intricacies so deli-
> cate and ingenious, so strict and artful, so
> involved and interlaced, and illuminated with
> colours still so fresh, that verily you would say

these were all combined by the diligence of an angel rather than of a man. For my part, the more often and carefully I look upon it, I am ever astonished anew: I ever find food for wonder.

But we possess one art treasure that can bring the *Book of Kildare* more vividly to mind than this description by Giraldus Cambrensis. I mean the *Book of Kells.* He who desires to commune with the spirit of Celtic Christianity, to find across the gulf of centuries some point of mental contact with Brigid, should not fail to repair to the library of Trinity College, Dublin, and, with a magnifying glass, study the *Book of Kells* for half an hour. It is just such another as the lost *Book of Kildare,* and the description of one applies almost equally to the other.

The average reader cannot read the *Book of Kells,* of course. Apart from the language, a calligraphic preparation would be necessary. But all may look at it and admire. Examine the most famous of the illuminations, the "Christus" monogram. This has been magnified by means of a projecting lantern to about three thousand times its size, and even such a searching test could discover no defect in the work. The spirit of the Celtic monasteries exhales from such pages. Think of the minds, gay, devout, often whimsical, that conceived these pictures, and the inexhaustible skill and patience of the hands that executed them. From the *Book of Kells* the artists' free access to beauty speaks eloquently; their attunement to harmony; their humble gratitude for the Gospel; their abiding and vital love of the Gospel. The records of the period tell of one great personage, Columcille, who particularly loved this work of illuminating because it helped him to meditate. By some secret nexus the skilful restraint imposed on the hand released the mind. He would throw out a bold and imaginative capital to some such sentence as this, attributed to him in the *Book of Kells*: *"Nolite thesaurizare vobis thesauros in terra,"* and then, in stippling on the crimson, blue, yellow, green and jet, his soul soared. And as he shaded in and dotted the interlaced bands, the foliage, spirals, and reptilinear convolutions, he was travelling in a far country. Look long at the *Book of Kells*. The atmosphere it evokes is the atmosphere of the Brigidine settlements.

The writer of the earliest Latin life of Brigid, Cogitosus, who wrote his account in the seventh century, gives us a description of the church of Kildare as it was in his day, that is before the Scandinavian horror had clawed the heart out of the Celtic shrines. The description is very often quoted, being of great historical value for a number of reasons. We are accustomed to think

of the monastic settlements as very poor and
bare, rudimentary in style and decoration,
whereas this passage indicates their occasional
richness. Cogitosus tells us that in his day the
tombs of Brigid and Conlaeth were at the right
and left, respectively, of the high altar in the
church of Kildare; the two shrines were lavishly
decorated with silver, gold, and gems; a crown
of gold hung over Brigid's tomb, and a crown
of silver over Conlaeth's, both crowns being
suspended from the roof. He tells us, moreover,
that the church was very spacious and lofty,
with a richly decorated interior. A rood-screen
of tapestry and paintings extended before the
high altar, and there was a door at each end
of the screen. Through the right-hand door the
priest and his assistants entered the sanctuary
for the celebration of Mass; and through the
left-hand door the nuns were wont to come before the altar for Holy Communion. The laity
were divided by means of a high partition running down the nave, and there were two en-
trances—one for women, the other for men. In
this way monks, nuns, and laity could worship
in the church together, yet apart and in privacy.

Cogitosus wrote between the years 620 and
680, roughly about one hundred years after the
passing of Brigid. Even in her time the church
must have been rich, for the period. Its pros-

perity was not, as in so many cases, a danger to
it, for the presence of a bishop and clergy in an
adjoining settlement gave it protection. Nothing
now remains of that ancient splendour. The
sole memorial of the holy city of Kildare is the
Round Tower, which does not date from St.
Brigid's time; it is remarkable for its great
height, rising one hundred and thirty-seven
feet—and for a doorway of graceful and beautiful ornamentation.

The tower looks out across the grassy expanse
of the Curragh, nearly five thousand acres of
undulating pasture. The right of commonage
for grazing sheep on this great unenclosed common originated with Brigid and has been preserved since her day. Along those lovely green
vistas she drove so frequently that the tradition
of her passing is still vividly alive there after
fifteen hundred years. The white figures of the
timid sheep at their peaceful grazing are her
real memorial. To the imaginative the bleat of
a sheep as dusk is falling instantly evokes the
rumble of her chariot-wheels and the sense of
her benediction descending on the land.

SIX

The Brigidine School of Mystics

THE texture of St. Brigid's story is threaded with great names. Every outstanding personage in the Irish ecclesiastical world of her day began to seek her out within a few years of her profession in order to profit by her counsel. They put their problems before her and accepted her solution. In this manner probably the first school of mystics of which we have knowledge began spontaneously to form around her.

St. Finnian belonged to that group of the spiritual élite. He was of Leinster stock like Brigid and founder of Clonard, the only school in Ireland that then outrivalled Kildare. He was a famous administrator, having as many as three thousand students together at the same time in his school and one hundred teachers in charge of them. He was known to his contemporaries as "Tutor of the Saints of Ireland."

Fiacc, Bishop of Sletty, was another of her friends. He is one of the most interesting personages in Celtic Ireland. On the Easter Sunday morning of 432, when St. Patrick was summoned before Laoghaire at Tara, Fiacc was only a boy, under-study to the Chief Poet of Erin, and thereby entitled to stand in the royal retinue. He was one of the first converts to Christianity and was baptized by Patrick. As he had acquired the photographic memory of a poet, he distinguished himself by learning the whole Catechism in one night. He wrote a metrical life of St. Patrick, still treasured as one of the most important Patrician documents extant.

Brigid's circle also included Ailbe of Emly, who wrote one of the first monastic Rules in Church history. A great Northern chieftain, too, brought his son to Kildare for baptism, asking Brigid to choose a name and make a prophecy about the babe. This child was Tigernach, who afterwards became second Bishop of Clogher and founder of the school of Clones. The link with Kildare determined his whole life. St. Kevin, also a Leinster man, took Brigid's advice in his boyhood. The fame of his monastery and school at Glendalough is further testimony of her influence.

Brendan the Navigator is one of the strangest names in her circle. What could such as he learn

from the cloistered nun? This explorer was so
unsubdued by fear that he could face the seven
seas in a hide-covered coracle. His face tanned
from exposure, his eyes keen from piercing long
distances, he must have been—to say the least—
an unusual figure among the convent guests.
He visited Kildare on his return from one of his
distant and mysterious voyages, when his coracles
were beached and his companions safely housed
again. Brendan seems to have been of such self-
sufficing austerity, so independent of that need
felt by all men—communion with their kind—
that he chose for his oratory an inaccessible
mountain peak, over three thousand feet above
sea-level, where the winds from the Atlantic
constantly whirl! It is really rather surprising
to find this indomitable explorer, who was
more practised in seamanship than in conversation with nuns, this restless adventurer for God,
this most audacious of the saints, admitting that
he had something to learn from Brigid. Only a
tantalizing fragment of their exchanges is given
in the "Lives." Brendan's purpose in visiting
her was to ask how she prevailed so powerfully
with God. Clearly he was intrigued by the things
he had heard of her. He asked her so little, yet
so much; one mystic taking counsel with another. Brigid told him with simplicity that it
was because her mind was never detached from

God. Is this the Illuminative Way that mystical writers, centuries later, endeavoured so laboriously to explain?

In all that is recorded of Kildare, this fact emerges as an enduring tribute to Brigid and her associates: there is no word of trouble there of any kind. The first shadow that fell on Kildare was cast by hostile lay forces, closing in upon it from the outside world, intent on plunder. Not the faintest breath of scandal ever touched the double monastery founded by Brigid and Conlaeth.

As Dom Gougaud observes:

> The best explanation that has been offered of the phenomenon is that such an organization had no chance of surviving save in an extremely pure spiritual atmosphere, and this the influence of the Irish monks of that age was certainly likely to produce.

A feature of this period of Celtic Christianity was the ideally friendly co-operation between all the first monastic settlements: there was no futile rivalry between them, but rather a loving spirit of collaboration. The life of St. Columcille in particular abounds in examples of the affection that linked together all the early monastic founders. When one visited the settlement of the other, he was always received "with honour and with joy." They exchanged gifts; they entertained each other with modest festivities. A special "brotherhood" was sometimes established between two or more monasteries, according to the terms of which the members of one community shared in the merits of the other; and one settlement would be pledged to defend the other in time of danger. Not until one hundred years after the death of St. Brigid is there any question in the Annals of discord between monks. This cordial spirit of unity flowed out to include the first convent settlements for women. Thus the mystical fellowship inspired by Brigid was the natural expression of early Irish monasticism.

Not only great Christian leaders were welcomed by Brigid, but the humblest layfolk too. Girls especially seem to have flocked to her. Not all these were aspirants to convent life. Many of them were fixed in their choice of a secular state, but nevertheless they were powerfully drawn to the saint. One girl of the many who visited Brigid found that the hours had passed by in a flash, and she was exceedingly sorrowful when it was time to go. "Stay here for the night," said Brigid. "But there is no one at home to milk the cows," the girl answered, "no one to feed the calves, or drive in the cattle, unless I go." "Leave all that to me," said Brigid. So the girl, persuaded, stayed the night in the convent. Of course, when she got home next day, all her property was safe and all her tasks had been done for her by miracle.

Another girl's heart seemed to break when the moment of departure came. "Stay here for the night," said Brigid the hospitable. But this girl had an aged paralysed father waiting at home and she insisted with anguish that she should return, or his anxiety would be intolerable. "Leave all that to me," said Brigid. When the girl returned home in the forenoon of the following day, her father welcomed her with a tranquil smile. He said the sun had never ceased shining during her absence, which he believed to have lasted but an hour. That is a pleasing picture of the old man, dozing off in the sunshine, his eyes sealed at Brigid's prayer, so that he was spared the torturing passage of lonely hours, and awaking to see the sun still shining and his daughter coming towards him.

Brigid's emblem in Ireland to-day is a cross woven of rushes, or straw, and the custom still persists in many districts of weaving these crosses on the eve of her feast-day and hanging them inside the eaves of the houses to invoke her blessing on the homes and land. The emblem and the custom take their origin in the story of how she once brought about the conversion of a pagan chieftain, who lived in the neighbourhood of Kildare. This man was dying and some Christian in his household sent for Brigid. When she arrived, the chieftain was raving. It is hardly possible to instruct a delirious man, so hopes for his conversion were diminishing. Brigid sat down at his bedside and began by consoling him. As was customary in that age, the floor was strewn with rushes both for warmth and cleanliness. It was a floor covering easily renewed. Brigid reflectively stooped down and picked a bunch of rushes from the floor at her feet; she started to weave them into a cross by fastening the points together. The sick man asked her what she was doing. She began to explain the Cross, and as she talked his delirium quietened down and he questioned her with growing interest. He believed and was baptized at the point of death. That is the reason why the primitive cross of rushes has been venerated in Ireland for fifteen hundred years. Moreover, the Irish carry this custom around the world with them. I saw the rush cross behind the door of a Boston apartment last year.

How is one to account, even from the human standpoint, for the fascination exercised by Brigid? It is evident that she had that quality, rare and excellent in woman, brevity of speech. She was, too, a great lover of good cheer. By which I do not mean she practised an occasional hospitality that was rich and lavish, but a perpetual hospitality that was good-humoured. There is a hymn attributed to her which represents her as imagining the details of the great banquet that is life everlasting. One item in that list gives a key to her character, this: I should like cheerfulness to be in their drinking.

Dourness and Brigid must be eternally dissociated. Neither in the sayings attributed to her, nor in her actions, can one find the faintest hint disapproving the recreations of ordinary men. She appears to have insisted on gaiety.

She was a lover of music. There is a story told of how she called one day at a chieftain's fortress, somewhere near Knockaney, in County Limerick, to plead with him for the liberation of a captive. The chieftain was out and his aged foster-father told Brigid and her companions to sit down and wait for his return, which was not likely to be prolonged. They did so. Brigid examined her surroundings and her eyes fell on harps hanging from the wall, as was the custom in Celtic homes. She smilingly asked for some music. But they told her the harpists were out, too, with the master and that they who remained had not the skill.

One of the nuns suggested that the men should try to play and that Brigid would give

them the gift. "She can do anything," the sisters
explained. A man who was foster-brother to the
absent lord took down a harp reluctantly and,
with what a foolish grin can be imagined,
thrummed it with clumsy fingers. But he, who
had never played, found he could produce airs,
and harmony issued! Absorbed in the novelty
he sat down with the instrument and began to
play the music with which his Celtic soul was
filled. Another of the household excitedly tried
on a second harp—with the same result.

Presently the pair were harmonizing with
great beauty and effect, the air vibrating with
old laments, epics and songs of victory. The
nuns were vastly entertained.

When the chieftain came home he found a
concert in progress. Lovely strains were floating
from his dun, with sounds of applause and mer-
riment. He heard the rare laughter of his aged
foster-father. Pleased with this home-coming,
he conceded to Brigid all that she asked.

These qualities, brevity of speech, love of
good cheer and music, partly account—at least
from the human standpoint—for the fascination
exercised on her contemporaries by Brigid. She
rallied about her in particular all the great in
the land who pursued holiness in an intelligent
way. Far too little attention has been paid to
the significance of this movement she almost

unconsciously initiated. Its enormous and abiding influence on the national stamp of character
may, perhaps, be overlooked. Nine hundred
years were to elapse before anything resembling
the Brigidine group was to appear on the Con-
tinent of Europe, when at length its counterpart
was seen in the cenacolo of Catherine Benincasa,
later called St. Catherine of Siena, whose
"Family" preceded all the famous salons of
Europe. It was one hundred years after that
before a woman, in the person of the "divine"
poetess, Vittoria Colonna, proved again that she
could be at once leader and inspiration of an
intellectual rebirth. In France there was nothing
resembling such feminine initiative until the
seventeenth century; and in England nothing
that recalled it until the nineteenth century. But
not to incur the charge of bathos, it would be
better, perhaps, not to mention in the same
breath with the Brigidine circle Madame
Récamier's salon, or the "intellectual after-
noons" of Hannah More and George Eliot.

Very surprising is the discovery that the feminine inspiration which delighted Europe in
later centuries down to modern times was
already an accepted feature of the early Irish
Church. But what particularly distinguished the
Brigidine School of Mystics from all faint or

imaginable counterparts was its charming pastoral character.

The Irish "Life" preserved in the *Leabhar Breac* describes the encounter between the nun, Brigid, and the navigator, Brendan, in one line that is a perfect idyll: *She came from her sheep to welcome Brendan.* Before Brigid died we are told she was the Mother Abbess of thirteen thousand nuns. One would have expected a personage of such importance to have been discovered at some more impressive employment: seated on a rostrum, perhaps, haranguing her community, or exhorting them; or at a desk before a manuscript, with a quill pen in her hand. But all Brigid's recreations from work are told in that line. Her shelter, where her strength was secretly renewed, where her soul was annealed in the murmurous quiet, was solitude in the green fields under the open sky. Hence that picture of Arcadian beauty and simplicity: *She came from her sheep to welcome Brendan.*

St. Brigid is supremely the saint of agricultural life. She is the genius of our Irish homesteads, and every farm is in a sense her shrine. She is the tutelar spirit of meadows and gardens. Throughout all her career, she was never dissociated from farmwork. She is found milking cows and making firkins of butter, rounds of cheese, and tubs of home-brewed ale until the end. Not even when she was Mother Abbess of all the nuns of Ireland did she relinquish her rural occupations: we still find her coming in from shepherding, her garments saturated with rain; or supervising reapers from dawn to sunset in the fields around her convent settlement. The Irish missionaries who went to Europe in the succeeding centuries carried with them the enthusiastic cult of Brigid and gained for her immense popularity in all the countries they evangelized. But the pastoral character of her cult remained unchanged. Her feast-day on February 1st ushers in the springtime, and her blessing was always invoked that day on the crops, the flocks and the herds.

Yet remember the famous school of which she was guiding spirit. There is an ancient statue of her in the little chapel of SS. Drédeneaux, in the parish of Géran, near Pontivy, Brittany, in which she is represented as holding a book in one hand and a quill pen in the other. For she was the patroness of learning too and fostered culture equally with pastoral pursuits.

The Gaelic tradition derives directly from Celtic Christianity. Brigid teaches us to associate words that have since become wrongly dissociated in the iron age of industrialism. She was an intellectual dairymaid, a cowherd with

culture, a field-labourer promoting art and literature, a shepherdess who had learning. In
considering Brigid at her farmwork, let this
statement in the *Book of Lismore* be held in
mind too:

> Wherefore thence it came to pass that the
> comradeship of the world's sons of reading is
> with Brigid, and the Lord gives them through
> Brigid's prayer every perfect good they ask.

SEVEN

The Bounty of Brigid

IN ANY attempt to understand St. Brigid's out-look two matters arising from her charity must be disposed of first: that charge so frequently made against her of exceeding the limits of prudence in her bounty—it was said her reckless giving was in fact a failing rather than a virtue; and secondly, those sentiments imputed to her in a certain interesting poem.

It is clear that Brigid's relatives, if none other, believed all through her life that she verily did push almsgiving to such lengths that she con-fused it with injustice. Even the highest virtue takes on very easily in prejudiced minds the colouring of error. Probably the purest happi-ness known to Brigid was the dispensing of charity; but this happiness always appears to have been diminished by a querulous voice raised in criticism, somewhat like the complain-

ing voice of Judas against the prodigality of
Mary Magdalen.

The stories that would illustrate this position
of affairs are numerous, but here only a brief
selection can be offered. It has been told how
Brigid's stepmother believed the girl could not
distinguish between charity and actions that
amounted to injustice towards her father; the
stepmother even persuaded Dubthach to this
belief. In fact all the trials of Brigid's life before
she became a nun arose from conflict between
her view of just almsgiving and the view taken
by others. What is more unusual, however, is
that this conflict and its consequent trials continued even in the cloister.

It would be useless to evade the fact that
Brigid, in her championship of the poor, made
heavy demands upon the patience of her friends.
Or put it like this; the poor and the afflicted
were her greatest friends, and for their sakes she
disappointed everyone. Even the nuns objected
to her methods. There is a story that when some
ecclesiastical dignitaries were due to visit her,
the community took pains to prepare a feast
worthy of the event. They scraped, planned,
contrived, and at last, on the eve of the great
day, all was in readiness. Then a host of beggars
came swarming to the gates. Brigid spoke to
them, and saw their plight at a compassionate

glance. Hastening to the larder, and quite un-mindful of her community's embarrassment, she distributed that carefully gathered feast among the mendicants, even down to the last crumb.

Another story tells us how she would take upon herself even the fatigue of the poor. One day she and some of her nuns set out on a long journey in two cars. On their way, they encoun-tered a man and his family toiling along under heavy burdens, evidently moving house. Noth-ing would satisfy Brigid but to jump from her car, making her nuns alight also, and offer the vehicles to this poor family. Then she and her sisters sat by the roadside to consider their posi-tion. They could not proceed on foot, because the distance was too great. I purposely omit the end of these episodes in order to emphasize the bountiful nature of Brigid. But you are not to suppose that her nuns always rose easily to her heroic height, or even obeyed her without effort.

Once the Queen of Leinster presented her with a chain of considerable value; it was a pretty trinket, having a representation of the human figure carved in precious metal attached to one end, and a silver apple on the other end. Of course Brigid did not quite know what to do with it, but her nuns were pleased. They liked to accumulate some few treasures against a season of greater poverty, or for the enriching of their church, or for the extension of the convent. When Brigid saw their pleasure in the gift she gave it to them to store away. But later she chanced on the hiding place. Then there came to her gates the inevitable leper mendicant at a moment when she had nothing to give, and she gave him the chain! What is of special interest in this story is the nuns' attitude when they discovered what she had done. "They said to her with anger and bitterness: 'Little good have we from thy compassion to everyone, and we ourselves in need of food and raiment.'"

Another story tells of Conlaeth, Bishop of Kildare, going to Rome during his term of office and bringing back a set of vestments, of precious material and richly embroidered, for worthy compliance with the ritual on great feast-days. But he did not long enjoy them. Brigid, who had access to the sacristy, when next importuned by beggars at a period when her stores were low, laid depredatory hands on the Bishop's treasured possession—and gave it away! In other words she had weighed only two things: the alleviation of human misery against dignity of worship, and had made her choice. But would that have been Conlaeth's choice, and can one imagine that he was pleased?

Her charity was a source of chagrin not only

to her community but to her friends. Once a lady brought her a gift of choice apples, carefully selected and packed. As usual, a group of lepers were congregated in the vicinity, and Brigid, opening her basket, immediately distributed the apples among them. "I did not bring them for those lepers," cried the visitor indignantly, "but for you." "What is mine is theirs," answered Brigid.

Like all who are openhanded, she was occasionally victimized by what today are called "undeserving cases." Like all liberal givers, too, she was heavily censured for those known instances of victimization that seemed to justify her critics. I do not believe that Brigid really was deceived, or that her discernment of souls failed at such junctures. Punishment always followed those who defrauded her. It is probable that she preferred to maintain the principle of bounty even when she detected a cheat. And very often the sweetness of her charity effected the conversion of those who essayed to dupe her.

Once a smart young man in comfortable circumstances, who thought Brigid a fool, assumed the disguise of a pauper and went whining to her for alms. He found her in the fields shepherding and begged a sheep from her flock. She gave him one. Elated by success, the smart young man drove the sheep to his own pen, assumed

a different disguise, and once more joined the
beggars that were always swarming around
Brigid. Again she gave the impostor a sheep.
He played the same trick on her seven times in
succession, and that night, although tired from
his journeys, he laughed much over the addi-
tional sheep in his pen. But next morning they
were missing! All gone, leaving never a trace
of their passage, while Brigid's flock was increased by the addition of seven sheep. And the
laugh turned against the smart young man who
had spent such a laborious and futile day.

The "Lives" are crowded with kindred stories
of Brigid turning the tables, and many of the
incidents are distinctly humorous. Once, two
robbers stole some cattle from her fields at nightfall. Things went well until they reached a river
that had to be forded and here the cattle became
stubborn. Nothing would induce them to cross.
All night long the thieves, whacking and shouting, strove with the recalcitrant animals, but to
no avail. The men took counsel and at daybreak
decided on a plan. Taking off their clothes,
which they tied to the animals' horns, they
plunged into the river and pulled the cattle after
them with ropes. This method worked until they
were in midstream. Then the cattle broke from
the ropes, made back to the bank, and galloped
home with all speed, the clothes still tied to their

horns. When the sun rose, the farmfolk going to work were diverted by the spectacle of naked men racing desperately a long, long way behind the flying cattle. And the people were "wondrously amazed."

Another day, Brigid saw passing her cashel gates a man with a sack on his back. She surmised that he carried salt, then a coveted luxury. "What have you on your back?" she said. "Stones," said the churl, who feared she might want some of his salt. "Stones let it be," said Brigid. And at once the man's spine appeared to buckle under the new weight and he found himself curved double under his load. He stumbled back to this Mother Abbess whose word was so fearful. "What have you in that?" said Brigid. "Salt," he answered. "Salt let it be," she said. And immediately it was salt, and he gave her some for the community.

Of course not all Brigid's contemporaries were thus niggardly toward the great Mother Abbess. On the contrary, her generosity inspired the same response in others. She was returning one day from a distant missionary journey with some companions when night overtook them while they were still a long way from Kildare; actually they were only halfway between Drogheda and Dublin. They were forced to stop at a poor house and ask for a night's hospitality. They got a delightful welcome. The woman ran to receive them with open arms and began to praise and thank God for the honour done to her house. A new-born calf was immediately killed for the guests, and when fuel ran short the woman broke up her distaff so as to make a good fire. A distaff was the coveted possession of every woman of the period, ranking first in feminine riches. It need hardly be said that Brigid noted these sacrifices with a sympathetic eye and that the story ended happily. Next day a calf was replaced with the cow, and we are told that the cow liked it as much as if it were her own, and the good woman who had so generously received the nuns was presented with a new distaff.

But, not to digress too widely, did Brigid herself as a fact push charity beyond its bounds to the point where begins the first faint injustice to others? From the purely human standpoint, it would look almost like that, but since she is a saint of the Church, one is not permitted to suppose that her charity was indiscriminate, or that she was likely to confuse any moral values. We must rather believe, however unpalatable the idea, it is our own religious perceptions that are blunted and confused, and hers that were acute and clear. In this matter of almsgiving, though she appears to the average eye to have sailed very close to the wind, her actions were in fact calculated with fine precision. And what we have to do is to enlarge, however painfully, our narrow and mean outlook to the measure of her nobility. Observe in the foregoing stories how invariably she placed the relief of distress before all other considerations. Second, and a long way second, was the maintenance of family status, the dignity of her position, her own well-being, the comfort of her community, grandeur of the ritual, splendour of her churches, consideration of her friends, and even her personal repute for discernment. For all these things she cared, of course, but she cared more for the poor. Her heart was always with the despised of this world. As for herself, she possessed nothing. There is a sense in which she is the mightiest democrat, the greatest of Christian communists. But so radical was her method, it cannot even be studied in this way without ill-ease. What the story of her life emphasizes above all else is charity, but it is a kind of charity that is full of hard sayings.

The curious poem attributed to Brigid is preserved in a manuscript of the Brussels library, and O'Curry believed it to be of such antiquity that it existed in the time of Aengus, that is about the end of the eighth century. This is O'Curry's prose translation of the poem (Gaelic

poetry suffers sadly when thus translated directly
into English):

I should like a great lake of ale
For the King of the kings.
I should like the family of Heaven
To be drinking it through time eternal.
I should like the viands
Of belief and pure piety,
I should like flails
Of penance at my house.
I should like the men of Heaven
In my own house;
I should like kieves
Of peace to be at their disposal.
I should like vessels
Of charity for distribution.
I should like caves
Of mercy for their company.
I should like cheerfulness
To be in their drinking;
I should like Jesus,
Too, to be there (among them).
I should like the three
Marys of illustrious renown;
I should like the people
Of Heaven there from all parts.
I should like that I should be
A rent-payer to the Lord;
That, should I suffer distress,
He would bestow upon me a good blessing.

It would be practically impossible at this date to establish with certitude the authorship of this poem. But a question of greater interest is whether the sentiments it expresses are at variance with our knowledge of Brigid. One of the many commentators thought so; or, at any rate, he disliked the poem. "One would imagine," he protested, "that the Eternal was a soma-quaffing deity." But that is to miss the point.

Brigid's sole recreation was hospitality. Everyone who came to her doors was entertained. In this lavish dispensing, her only disturbing thought was fear lest supplies should be insufficient. Would the butter last out? And would the bread go round? These were the misgivings of Brigid, the hostess. All earthly repasts come to an end. This great-souled woman was always sorry to see her guests departing. Had they had enough? and would they be hungry tomorrow? were her solicitudes.

In a note at the commencement of the Litany of Aengus, reference is made to a Synod held in Munster under Bishop Ibar, and Brigid's poem is mentioned in connection with this assembly. In those metrical lines therefore, the saint is imagined describing the ideal feast that should fittingly follow such a distinguished conference. And it is not so much that Brigid would like a great lake of ale for consumption by the King of kings; her concept rather is that a feast presided over by the Lord of all should, in justice to its character, be replenished from inexhaustible supplies and, in fact, go on for ever.

Brigid was familiar with ale-vats drained dry, or, at her fervent prayer, mysteriously refilled for some exhausted wayfarers, but she never knew a condition of life in which ale-vats were standing full against a time of need. She never had enough for those who came to her gates. She was always going hopefully to a larder she knew to be empty, to a dairy she knew to be deplenished, even to cows that she knew had been already milked. Her ideal feast then, worthy of the Host and satisfying to Himself, would naturally include as its first item, "a great lake of ale."

I fear that this emphasis on ale may distress the reader who persists, despite my warnings, in reading the twentieth century into the fifth. Perhaps he already sniffs in those Celtic synodal gatherings the pungent atmosphere of a saloon-bar; he may even hear the repeated clink of glasses, and is probably now formulating animadversions.

Ale, let it be explained, was brewed from malt in every household, even the poorest, of that period. It was the practice to store the barley-malt, usually in cakes, which would keep for any length of time. Ale was the universal drink and was always offered to visitors in much the same way as a cup of tea is offered now. Being hardly fermented, its intoxicating properties were negligible. One need not, therefore, grudge the Celtic monks their ration of ale. Its qualities can hardly have been good in the modern sense, for it has been equated to whey. Our modern tea is probably a more stimulating and a far less wholesome beverage than the fifth-century ale.

At this ideal banquet of Brigid's, then, not only should the refreshment be drawn from inexhaustible supplies, so that the host might be happy in a guarantee against discomfiture, but the guests should be innumerable, and the feasting should go on for ever without any diminution of enjoyment. No one should have a care at that table, as is expressed in the great line: *I should like cheerfulness to be in their drinking*. For all that, they should be men familiar with mortification, and who, therefore, understood temperance, too, and restraint. All the virtues in fact would be found among those happy guests: belief, piety, peace, charity, mercy. And Brigid's large-heartedness is expressed even in the very amplitude of the containers she is supposed to enumerate: there would be even kieves of peace and caves of mercy.

Whatever about the real authorship of the poem, it is correct to ascribe such sentiments to Brigid. How correct will not be understood unless her hospitality be lifted on to the spiritual plane where it belongs. It must be noted that Brigid was not isolated in this devotion to strangers and the poor. The driving strength of the principle of hospitality among all the Celtic saints must be remembered. They truly believed that Christ was present in the person of the stranger, and especially when the person was poor. For this reason the best site within the monastic enclosure was reserved for the guest-house—it was one of the most important of the buildings—and a special tract of land was assigned for its maintenance. The most extreme examples of the sensitiveness of Irish saints in the matter of hospitality were Cronan, who transferred his whole monastery on finding that it was rather inaccessible to travellers: and Atracta, who would settle nowhere except at the junction of seven principal roads.

It is sometimes affirmed that the stamp of hospitality on the national character, that peculiarly Irish detestation of niggardliness, is derived from secular sources. True, the monastic family was, in all that concerned the distribution of offices and suchlike, a kind of model of a chieftain's household. This, in the case of the principal families, nearly always included an official known as the hospitaller, whose chief duty was to provide entertainment for travellers; while the lay lords' terror of incurring the blister of a poet's satire through any sign of stinginess often drove them to extravagant lengths in their hospitality. But that unfeigned solicitude for the stranger in their midst, that genuine love of the poor as "friends of heaven," without officialism or ulterior motive, which still distinguishes the Irish people, derives its full strength not from secular sources chiefly, but in larger part from the spiritual heritage of the Celtic saints.

EIGHT

"A Spray of Irish Fioretti"

Two collections of Christian literature—the Lives of the early Irish saints, and the Fioretti of St. Francis of Assisi—produce exactly the same effect on the mind. In the pages of both there live creatures utterly detached from the world, soaring triumphantly above our commonplace miseries. Both writings exhale the same candid charm while enforcing the same divine ideal.

The affinity between Celtic Christianity and the Franciscan movement is striking. True, a return to the simple life in religion is a stock principle of most reforming movements, but merely a common principle does not explain this special kinship. The Franciscan movement is described as an attempt to reproduce the primitive Church. But it might be described too as a reflorescence of the Celtic Church, of which it bore all the distinctive marks. Both the Celtic and the Franciscan saints expressed the same love of solitude and remote retreats; they manifested themselves in the same spiritual intimacy between men and women, the same exaltation of poverty, the same stress on heroic penance, always with the same artless simplicity, the same emphasis on manual labour, the same ardent loyalty to Rome. Little wonder that when the sons of St. Francis came to Ireland, their conquest was immediate. They found themselves on native soil.

The ancient Irish used to delight their children with tales of St. Ciaran and his woodland monks. Belonging, like Brigid, to the sixth century, he founded his church in a forest clearing, where he tilled and ploughed and prayed. He wore the dressed skins of animals, and every evening his dinner consisted of a small piece of barley-cake, two vegetable roots, and a drink of water. Presently the animals gathered in docility about him. First a boar, then a fox, later a badger, a wolf, and even a deer, with her fawn, came humbly to his side and, learning from him, trotted about all day under his guidance. He taught them to be useful.

But there came a day when the fox had a sad lapse. Finding the saint's sandals of soft, untanned hide lying about, he sniffed them curi-

ously. He had known the taste of such material;
besides he was hungry, for one was always fast-
ing in the monastic enclosure. Not yet schooled
to resist temptation, he stole the sandals and
made off with them to his old lair. When the
bad deed was discovered, Ciaran sent the badger
into the wood to look for the fox. The badger
knew where to go. He arrived at the fox's den
just as the delinquent, having eaten the laces
and the flaps, was about to enjoy the remainder
of his meal. But the monitor, flinging himself
on the fox, bit his ears and his tail, and pulled
his hair with violence, to bring him to his senses.
Then he led home the truant, carrying the
sandals. It was the ninth hour when they reached
Ciaran.

" 'Why have you done this wrong?' said the
saint mildly. 'Have you not yet learned to suffer
the need of food and drink?' But the fox doing
penance fasted for three days."

Seven hundred years later the Church pro-
duced just such another as Ciaran in the person
of Francis Bernardone, who, in far-off Umbria,
tamed the wolf of Gubbio. In his deep love of
nature, Francis acquired dominion over the
animal kingdom and he and his disciples seemed
to live again in the earthly Paradise. Even
unbelievers, irresistibly attracted to Francis,
concede that Franciscan lore has permanently

enriched the world's literature. Within the last few decades the Saint of Assisi has become fashionable, and his life has been written by sectarians of every imaginable kind. These sentimentalize endlessly over the less important, but perhaps the more charming, aspects of his life, whereas all our rich Celtic inheritance, so strikingly similar, is still for the most part secreted in difficult manuscripts and is to-day unknown in Ireland, even among admirers of St. Francis.

A genuine fioretto could be culled from the life of nearly every Celtic saint. Columcille—born two years before the death of Brigid and destined to become one of the greatest missionaries of his time, always ranked with Patrick and Brigid in Ireland's Great Triad—provides many such stories. One day, while he was living in the exile of Iona, a stork came flying out of the south from the direction of Ireland. Being badly beaten by the winds, it dropped from exhaustion on the beach. Columcille bade one of his monks lift up the bird with care and carry it to shelter. There it was nursed for three days and three nights, so that "refreshed, and with fully recovered strength, it might return to its former sweet home in Ireland, whence it came." Seven centuries later, Francis was to charm his contemporaries by expressing the same solicitude for the welfare of a few doves.

An analogous story tells of Columcille's contemporary, Colman MacDuach, who lived as a hermit in the desert. He trained in his service a cock, a mouse, and a fly. It was the cock's duty to warn the monk when it was time for matins, and at the shrill crow the good man always seized his Psalter. The mouse watched his sleep, and having been taught to allow but five hours, if the hermit did not wake in due time, the mouse would rub his ear to call him. And the fly would attend when Colman read his psalms and would rest on the line where he left off, to hold the place until he resumed. But a fly's life is brief, that of a mouse too, and even of a cock. For all his severe mode of living, Colman enjoyed a joke. When these faithful friends of his died, he wrote a jesting letter to Columcille, complaining of the death of his "flock," much as a farmer would lament the loss of his herd. And Columcille answered in the same mood of raillery, consoling Colman in his new-found poverty, for that "misfortune exists only where there is wealth."

It might be contended that no member of the bird kingdom can express the quality of contentment better than a duck. Neurasthenics should contemplate these fowl. Their fat, quick waddle, their emphatic, self-satisfied quacking, their busyness, their grace of flight, their confident surrender to water, tirelessly reiterate one thing, joy of being. It is told of Brigid that she was out in the fields one day, watching wild ducks disporting themselves. Greatly pleased with them, she called them, and swiftly they winged towards her. She spoke caressingly to them, covering them with her hands, and they stayed with her until she dismissed them. St. Francis, too, displayed the same power. Once, when he was preaching, the singing of swallows on the trees disturbed him, but when he told them to be silent, they obeyed. Another day he preached expressly to the birds, who remained motionless on the ground and on the nearby shrubs until he bade them go.

St. Brigid, like Ciaran, once tamed a fox. A bondman was cutting trees in a wood, when he unintentionally killed with his axe a fox that was crouching near him. Then it transpired that the animal was the King of Leinster's, a household pet, as domesticated as a dog and trained to perform a great number of useful and diverting tricks. The king was furious and, in his chagrin, would hear no explanations. The servant was thrown into captivity and his death decreed.

This news was brought to Brigid, who was asked to plead for the captive's life because she was known to have influence with the king. She set out at once in her chariot. On the way to the angry lord's fortress, she saw a fox peeping at her from a wood. She called it, and immediately it sprang into the car and nestled contentedly against her feet. Caressing it as she dismounted, she beckoned, and it trotted obediently behind her.

Within the fortress, she found the master indignantly obstinate. Nothing, he declared, could make up to him for the loss of his pet—and the blundering bondman should die. Brigid called forward the fox, fresh from the woods, and began to put it through clever tricks before a delighted household. The little animal that had never performed responded to her voice as though entranced, and did every manner of feat. Then she offered it in lieu of the prisoner's life, and the king, placated, agreed. When the bondman was liberated and guaranteed immunity from the threat of further punishment, Brigid returned to her convent. But the little fox missed its mistress and grieved for her whom instinct affirmed to be worthy of all trust. The moment attention was diverted, it made good its escape. The household flew to recapture it, "but the fox went safely back through the wood, the hosts of Leinster behind, both foot and horse, and hound."

Anciently, the monastic enclosure offered

asylum to all fugitives from justice. If they could gain it, they claimed "privilege of sanctuary," and were, with certain reservations, exempted from punishment. One would imagine that the animals knew this, for one day a wild boar, hotly pursued by hunters and on the point of collapse, plunged into Brigid's settlement. She received it into her herd of swine, where at once it lost its wildness and lived in peaceful domesticity for the remainder of its days.

This love of the animal kingdom and power over it, displayed both by the Celtic saints and the followers of Francis, had its common origin and its rational explanation. These saints, by renunciation and penance, regained that state of innocence in which man, completely master of himself, was master, too, over the animal kingdom. In the discipline that every saint is obliged to impose upon himself, he first seeks complete control over his emotional nature by denying it the legitimate satisfaction for which it craves. Yet they err who contend that the saints are not human. Their sensibility is not first deadened and then killed outright in this process of self-training. On the contrary, as the Abbé Joly has pointed out, it gains in ardour, in richness and delicacy. And instead of concentrating within narrow channels, the saints' affections extend

later in a divine outpouring to embrace all
creatures, and even to include all Creation.

Yet another brief story lights up this parallel
between Celtic Christianity and its Franciscan
counterpart. It will be remembered that Brigid
travelled around Ireland at a period when the
country was a shaking sod of domestic strife.
She used every exertion, resorted to every expedient her genius could devise, in order to
stem that useless, bitter flow of blood. One
instance was her intervention between Conall
and Cairbre—sons of the High Kings of Ireland
—who were disputing the boundaries of their
respective territories. So high ran the quarrel,
each determined to slay the other. On the day
the brothers set out with this evil purpose,
Brigid and her nuns encountered Conall and,
so resolved was she to prevent crime, she and
her sisters fell in behind his marching soldiery.
Their way lay "over the hills," which did not
make it easier for the nuns. Presently Cairbre's
band was seen approaching, and the sisters'
terror rose. What happened is not clear save for
two facts: there was no bloodshed, and the
brothers, with their armed escorts, mingled
peaceably in Brigid's company. It is said that
her prayers had drawn a film over their eyes, so
that they did not at first recognize each other.
Later they parted with a kiss. Certainly, through

the grace of Brigid's blessing, in more senses than one they did not know each other for the men they had been. Some time afterwards, Brigid achieved Conall's complete conversion and, though he did not cease from war, he one day cast off all his weapons and strewed them at her feet as a symbol that he had learned from her how to forgive injuries.

In her efforts to teach the turbulent chieftains of Ireland this hardest lesson of Christianity: that the greatest renunciation is the renunciation of revenge, Brigid's life would find its most adequate commentary in the Fioretti, where the supreme importance of free forgiveness is shown in a famous dialogue between Francis and Brother Leo on the subject of "perfect joy." Both were out walking, and for two miles of road the saint interrogated his companion on this question. Brother Leo learned progressively that "perfect joy" consists not in gladly suffering hardship, nor in the greatest miracles. Francis explained:

> If the Friars were to make the lame walk, if they could make straight the crooked, chase away demons, restore sight to the blind, give hearing to the deaf, speech to the dumb, and what is even a far greater work, raise the dead after four days, know that this would not be perfect joy.

And Francis went on to explain to Leo that perfect joy consists not in the knowledge of languages, nor in culture, nor in science, nor in the gift of prophecy, nor in the reading of souls, nor in the knowledge of stars, plants, or animals, nor in the gift of such preaching as would convert the world, but in this only, the supreme virtue: free forgiveness of injuries. And the reason? Because all other things are the gift of God, in which we cannot glory. But in no way so truly as in the free forgiveness of injuries does man shoulder the Cross, in which alone he may glory.

The Franciscan emphasis on obedience as the most heroic form of humility is found everywhere in the lives of the early Irish saints. Giotto was not the first to attach special importance to the manner of making an O. The standard test of obedience in the Celtic monasteries was that a scribe, when summoned, should drop his pen even in the middle of the letter O. For obedience is a greater thing than beauty of penmanship. The Celtic saints had an intense desire for unity and order and complete knowledge of the eternal secrets of perfection.

The analogy between Celtic Christianity and the Franciscan movement could be extended almost indefinitely. The parallelism between the incidents provided by the two is very striking.

Patrick is instructed by an angel, so is Brother Elias; Brigid washes a leper, so does Francis; Patrick fasts during the whole of Lent on the summit of Croagh Patrick, Francis does likewise on an island in the lake of Perugia; Brigid, believing that the dignity of church ceremonial is a secondary matter compared with relieving the poor, gives away Bishop Conlaeth's rich vestments; Brother Juniper, in the same frame of mind, cuts the bells off an altar-cloth and hands them to a beggar; Brigid heals leprosy, so does Francis; Brigid takes a meal with her clerical guests, St. Clare eats with Francis and his companions; Brendan converses with the denizens of the deep, Anthony of Padua preaches to the fishes.

An Italian writer on this theme, Fra Anselmo Tommasini, O.F.M., has recently pointed out yet deeper conformities. Only two movements in Christian history, the Celtic and the Franciscan, have expressed themselves with equal fervour in the three forms of religious life: the eremitical, the cenobitical, and the apostolic. Both movements held that community life is the safeguard against the peculiar perils incurred in the other two modes of religious service: the pitfall for the hermit being spiritual egoism and ascetical pride; that of the itinerant preacher being a scattering of his contemplative powers.

And these two groups alone were content with nothing less than a world mission, not in extent only, but in depth too; not geographically merely, but socially also.

Would it be extravagant to claim that Celtic Christianity was the secret inspiration of the Franciscan revival? If the latter is an attempt to reproduce the primitive Church, did the Franciscan founders in fact learn the details of the new way of life from the records of the Celtic saints who had migrated to Italy, whose traditions were still vividly alive and whose legends were current there in the thirteenth century? Interesting historical links in this conjectural chain may yet be discovered. Spiritually the case seems complete.

NINE

The Wisdom of Brigid

ONE of the secrets of Patrick's outstanding success as a missionary was his masterly solution of that evangelizing difficulty called the "adaptation" problem. Like St. Paul, he became "all things to all men for the sake of Christ." Everything in the native culture that could lawfully be preserved, he preserved. And imperceptibly, without friction, he grafted it on to the Christian culture, without loss to his converts, without any painful or violent breach in their traditions. Towards everything in native art and institutions that did not conflict with Christianity, he showed himself most sympathetic.

In this attitude and method, Brigid devotedly followed his example. A great light is thrown on her ways in that dialogue with Ailill, son of Dunlaing and King of Leinster. The story goes that she had gone to Ailill at her father's request, to obtain from the king permission for Dubthach to keep a certain sword which he held on loan.

This being the sole occasion when Dubthach reappears in Brigid's religious life, a brief digression may be pardoned here. The father's reappearance has a very special interest. It indicates first that friendly relations were maintained to the end between father and daughter, for Brigid here obeyed him, and in fact secured what he wanted. The incident enhances the probability of Dubthach's conversion. But it opens up yet another and more important avenue of likelihood. Brigid's influence on her contemporaries and on her century was enormous. A large part of this was due to her unique strength of character and organizing genius. But how much of it was due also to her father's support? A great deal, we surmise. He was one of the petty princes of Leinster, with wealth and arms at his command. It is quite evident from Brigid's authority and security that she was given full recognition by her kinsfolk, and this is difficult to understand, remembering that she was the daughter of a slave. It cannot be explained even on Christian grounds. But Dubthach's support, if accorded freely, perseveringly, and even aggressively, would explain it perfectly. The point I am trying to make is this: socially Brigid acted as though she had the status of a Leinster princess. Now, with the best will in the world, the Church could not have conferred this status on her, such was the force of custom in these matters among the Celtic Irish. It is even dubious whether Brigid could have acquired such a position through her own worth. But Dubthach could have secured it for her, and he probably did.

To return to Ailill. The persons in his household likely to be most interested in Brigid's presence at the dun were the bond-slaves, for the Abbess's compassion on their lot was common knowledge. While she waited for the master, one of the slaves—a man—saw an opportunity to approach her. He implored her to procure his manumission, probably revealing to her all his pitiful experience. Brigid promised. She had then two requests to make of Ailill: her father's and the slave's. When at last the warrior saw her, he was disposed to bargain. He asked her, "Why should I give you all that?"

Although we know that Dunlaing was a Christian, it does not appear likely that his son, Ailill, had been at this period baptized. Anyhow Brigid readily promised him that her friendship would secure for him: excellent children, kingship for his sons, and ultimately the Kingdom of Heaven for himself.

But Ailill seemed little attracted by these

promises. I like the candour of the old heathen's reply:

> The Kingdom of Heaven, as I see it not, and as no one knows what thing it is, I ask it not. Kingship for my sons, moreover, I ask not, for I myself am still alive and let each one serve his time. But give me rather length of life in my realm and victory over the Ui Neill in battle.

Here one would imagine this should be the signal for Brigid to begin a sermon on the truths of eternal life; or a rebuttal of all the pagan philosophy implied in the ruler's cynical answer. But prudence forbade antagonizing him at that juncture. Another soul was in jeopardy, the slave's, who had vowed to enter Brigid's service if she procured his release. How Brigid's gifts of brevity and wisdom shine in her answer: "It shall be given."

Another story emphasizes Brigid's adaptability and practical common sense. One day in Lent, because of the previous harvest having failed, her community found themselves on the brink of starvation. Being forced to make some provision, Brigid set out with two of the sisters to visit a neighbouring monastery, then in charge of Ibar, and beg from him the loan of a supply of corn. The distance between the two churches was great and the nuns arrived exhausted and famished at the monastery. Famine was prevalent in the district. A meal—all that was available, bread and bacon—was set before the guests, and Brigid thankfully began on it. Presently she noticed that her two nun-companions were pointedly refraining from the bacon. There was a sniff in their attitude, implying, "Well, we're going to keep Lent, anyhow, whatever you do."

Not to avail of dispensation accorded under circumstances of such stress was really more than Brigid could stand. Rebuking the nuns sharply and with vehemence, she even turned them out of the room! In all the mass of legendary stories and traditions concerning Brigid, this is the sole instance recorded where she displayed anger. What provoked it is worth remembering: pharisaical formalism masquerading as piety.

One of the most distinctive traits of Brigid's character was her large and genial sympathy with average human nature. She not only felt for the ordinary ruck of men; she felt with them. She identified herself with them. Only an awkward word describes this characteristic, humanness. It was as far removed from frigid philanthropy as her burning charity was remote from the watery benevolence that is its modern official substitute.

There are innumerable stories in the "Lives" illustrating her human sympathy. The difficulties of labouring men touched her particularly and she never failed to respond to their appeal. On one occasion some workmen were cutting down a huge tree in the woods near Kildare. The timber was needed for some extension of the convent building. The men toiled for several hours to fell the tree, but when at last the giant toppled over, it came to rest in an awkward position from which their best efforts could not dislodge it. They brought oxen and ropes to the spot, as well as more men, but all their united efforts could not budge the tree. Finally they appealed to Brigid, and immediately the tree became movable.

Brigid's human sympathy is seen even in the very employments of her choice in that period of her life when she was free to choose. She knew the labour of milking cows in the early morning and at evening. She was familiar with the backache caused by the churn and with the perspiring heat of much breadmaking. She drove sheep along the road. She helped in the fields with the harvest. Her particular brand of home-brewed ale appears to have been famous. This means that she did not disdain to stoop for hours over malt-vats and tubs of mash. One of the feats recorded of her is that she supplied the seventeen churches in Meath with sufficient ale to last their little communities from Holy Thursday to Low Sunday.

It is worth remarking how all the saints appear to have applied themselves to menial work of the lowliest and most monotonous description. And the more exalted their natures became, the more they were favoured with inner light, then the more assiduously did they abase themselves in such toil. It was as though they were bent on establishing some secret and delicate equipoise, intuitively understood but not demonstrable. Mysticism appears to be fostered rather than disturbed by lowly offices. As well as teaching the dignity of manual labour, Brigid knew its use as a strong defence against *accidia* (of which the modern translation is "the dumps").

If a large part of Brigid's work was of the ordinary description, the alleviations she sought were ordinary too. Most interesting, because so unexpectedly illuminative of the period, is the frequent mention in the "Lives" of baths and bathing. She did not always cure leprosy through her miraculous gifts. She did this only under great compulsion, or out of compassion. She appears to have preferred assuaging the disease through human means, available to everyone, and in this curative treatment ordinary

washing figured largely. Many lepers, on going
to Brigid, were disappointed when, expecting
a miracle, they were faced with a bath.

Brigid favoured all the rigorous ascetic prac-
tices of the Celtic saints, among them cold-water
immersion in the winter. There is a story told
how on one particularly bitter night of winter,
she and a young companion immersed themselves in a pond. She thought this form of penance very beneficial and enthusiastically decided
to practise it every night. The following night,
when the two nuns went to the pond, they found
it dried up. The water welled up again the next
morning, but the following night the pond was
dry again. When the same phenomenon happened several nights in succession, Brigid understood that God did not wish her to practise this
penance. She resigned herself to continue her
spiritual formation without its help.

Unlike the majority of later saints, Brigid's
mode of life presents little requiring explanation, or even distasteful to ordinary men. It is
not the hagiographer's function to institute between the saints odious comparisons. Therefore
I draw no conclusions from the difference. I
merely state it by way of emphasizing Brigid's
humanness. What is not found in her life is in
its way nearly as remarkable as what is found
there. One reads no instance of levitation, no

ecstatic seizures, nothing far-fetched or startling in the way of revelation or prophecy, no marked eccentricities. We know solely from Brigid's achievements that she is to be isolated from her people and century; that she stands a solitary, arresting figure, unrelated to any cause, inexplicable. But she never expressed any self-consciousness of her singularity. Apart from her foundations, her miracles and organizing triumphs, she behaved like any nun of the fifth and sixth centuries, and even laboured away like any woman of her epoch.

I hope I shall not be misunderstood when I say Brigid prevailed powerfully with the heathen because she was as human as the heathen. That is to say, she never ignored those roots of our being that are common to all humanity. Before her splendour dawned in the morning of Celtic Christianity, the name Brigid was familiar to her people as that of a Druidical divinity, or mythical fire-goddess. A small section of the Brigidine literature is devoted to examining the affinity between the pagan and the Christian Brigid. A few fearfully dull books have even essayed to prove that there never was a real St. Brigid; that she was in fact merely a "survival" of the pagan deity. No one would waste time refuting this assertion, because it is not taken seriously. But the very character of

so many of the Brigidine miracles, trivial sometimes to the point of puerility, should have
warned the higher critics of their reality.

It is easy to point to the affinity between certain of the heathen legends and episodes in the
life of Brigid, but that affinity does not alone
suffice to destroy Brigid's historical truth. As a
matter of fact the vitality of the Christian saint
annihilates the dim concept of the pagan divinity. The abstraction fades before the bright-
ness of the concrete. The warm humanity of
Brigid that shines through the gossiping legends,
that flaming humanity, alternately vehement,
angry, tolerant, benign, completes before the
eye of the mind a living personality that is the
direct antithesis of the druids' cold and uncon-
soling myth.

TEN

The Tree of Love

ONE of the most appealing things told of Brigid is her contemporaries' belief that there was peace in her blessing. Not merely did contentiousness die out in her presence, but just as by the touch of her hand she healed leprosy, so by her very will for peace she healed strife and even cleansed the suppurating bitterness that foments it.

The same curious efficacy is attributed to Columcille's blessing, in the life so ably written of him by Adamnan, his successor in Iona. It was Columcille's habit to bless the monks, as they trudged wearily past his cell on their way home every evening from field-work. All the toilers experienced the same alleviation at the same moment and at the same place every evening. Since each of them thought his experience individual, no one spoke of this for a long while. But the moment they compared their experience they knew the origin of their strange inward renewal. The biographer tells us that this is how one of the monks described it, and the passage is a good example of Adamnan's manner:

> Some fragrance of marvellous odour, as of that of all flowers collected into one; also a certain burning as of fire, not painful, but as it were soothing; moreover too a certain accustomed and incomparable gladness diffused in my heart, which suddenly consoles me in a wonderful way, and gladdens me to such a degree that I can remember no more the sadness, nor the labour. Yea, even the load, although a heavy one, which I am carrying on my back from this place until we come to the monastery, is so lightened, I know not how, that I do not perceive I have a load at all.

The same effect was attributed to the blessing of Brigid, though not so well described in the writings concerning her. The passage might be taken, too, as giving Brigid's general effect on her contemporaries, to whom she seems to have been a source of the purest rejoicing. Here again she is most unlike later, and particularly modern saints, who usually appear to bear a heavy burden of misunderstanding, opposition, contemporary dislike and thwarting, and even hatred.

No burning enthusiasm for Brigid in later centuries could rival that of her own time. The sixth century loved her supremely. She is one of those rare cases of the prophet being accorded all honour in his own country; she was the seer who was not stoned; the patriot who was not sold. In a universal shout of acclamation, her own day ungrudgingly gave her her due. In this defeatist age, when the whole philosophy of failure is grossly distorted and exaggerated, usually for the assuaging of little minds; when every success has to be scrabbled together out of the ruins of some overthrow, neglect, or omission, the fact that the greatest Irishwoman of all time knew no defeat should have a tonic effect on the mind.

That intrepid voyager, Brendan, believed that Brigid's name was talismanic even among the very monsters of the deep. Columcille, in his exile at Iona, assuaged his grief of absence by penning her poetic praise. The missionaries, especially, carried Brigid's name everywhere like a banner of conquest. The *Book of Lismore* "Life" concludes with a hymn to Brigid. Some notion of what she meant to her own age can be gleaned from the anonymous writer's speculations about the authorship of this hymn. He makes five guesses: it might have been Columcille wrote it, when he was caught in Corry-vreckan whirlpool during a storm and prayed to Brigid for a calm sea; or it might have been Brocan Cloen, the seventh-century Abbot who certainly wrote an Irish hymn in her honour; or it might have been three of her disciples who went to Rome and told afterwards that when they found themselves in acute difficulties in a strange land, they prayed to her and received miraculous help; or it might have been Brendan, the Navigator, when he found her name honoured even by sea-monsters; or it might have been St. Ultan, Bishop of Ard-breccan, who was said to have written an alphabetical hymn in her honour.

The strength and the antiquity of St. Brigid's cult are attested by the ancient dedications to her scattered so numerously throughout Scotland, Wales, Cornwall, Devon, France, and particularly Brittany. All over western Europe too, in unexpected corners, the Irish traveller today is still electrified to stumble upon her shrine or chapel, with its familiar and eloquent message out of a remote past. Italy's devotion to two foreign saints, Brigid of Ireland and Brigid of Sweden, traces a sort of spiritual dividing line across the peninsula; the northern half honours the Irish saint, while the central and southern areas uphold the Swedish saint. In this southern land the Irish Brigid still retains her pastoral and agricultural character.

On one occasion in the fourteenth century, when Piedmont was suffering from hail-storms and frost for such a long period, it was feared there would be no harvest that year; St. Brigid was chosen as patron by the country people and mild weather returned. At Camerlata in the diocese of Como, there is a famous church dedicated to St. Brigid and said to date from the ninth century. Here her feast-day is still celebrated with exceptional fervour every year, drawing crowds of pilgrims from the surrounding territory.

In one respect Brigid was unlike her later counterpart, Francis, but very much like her great model, Patrick: we know nothing, or practically nothing, of the manner of her death. No record describing it is extant. Tradition says that the Last Sacraments were administered to her by Ninnid, called the Pure-handed, because while he was yet a boy, she had prophesied to him that he would have this privilege, and he had ever afterwards kept his right hand covered in token of the honour that was to be his. Being in Rome when she fell ill, he arrived back in Ireland to reach her bedside just in time. The day was February 1st, and the place where she died, Kildare. As near as can be ascertained, it was the year 524. Brigid was then only in the seventies, by no means an old woman, as age was reckoned in those days.

Cogitosus professed to describe Kildare in the sixth century, but he most probably described what he was looking at in the seventh century. We know from him that Brigid at first was laid to rest on the right-hand side of the high altar in her own church of Kildare; that, as has been said, her tomb was decorated with precious metal and jewels, and that a gold crown hung over it as a symbol of her sovereignty. This was in that Golden Age before horror of the Scandinavian sea-kings had been bred into the Irish chieftains. Later, in the year 835, for greater safety, her remains were removed to Downpatrick. Columcille's, too, were brought home from Iona. Patrick, Brigid, and Columcille were finally entombed together in the same grave in Downpatrick. During the vicissitudes of subsequent history, the identification of this grave was lost. It was miraculously re-discovered in the twelfth century. Today the position of this tomb is again doubtful.

On that hill where the Protestant Cathedral of Downpatrick frowns over the town, there is an ancient, somewhat unkempt and crowded graveyard. The inscriptions on the leaning or fallen headstones record that here lie buried men of an alien faith. A little way to the left of the entrance, overshadowed by the cathedral walls, there is a great block of uncut granite, irregular in shape, its highest part being some two feet above the ground. On the upper surface is incised a plain Roman cross, having, where the arms meet, a circle in the Celtic manner, signifying eternity. Under the cross there is cut in Irish characters the single word PATRIC. But the granite has been fractured at the end of the name, so that the C of the PATRIC is now missing. This, so far as our knowledge goes, is the grave of the National Apostle, and here lie buried with him, in the same dust, Brigid and Columcille. If they are not here, no man knows where they are. The granite block is not railed off or enclosed in any way; in fact, it is so closely hemmed in by graves, one finds difficulty in kneeling beside it.

The idea of a granite block for tombstone is striking in its simplicity. Patrick stands alone, without compeer or archetype. He is the one man in our history whose powerful name requires no eulogy, no date, no word from other men; there was only one Patrick. His mere name is his panegyric. No sculptor could further his fame; and in so far as he can be symbolized by a tombstone, a block of uncut granite from one of our mountains seems as fitting a monument as could be devised.

But otherwise the tragic unsuitability of this burial place strikes a chill on the heart. One would not care even to plead that Brigid and Columcille be mentioned on the tombstone; that is only the beginning of all that might be said on the subject. The temple of worship overshadowing the site is discordantly cold, empty and smelling of disuse. But the whole grievance is an old story now. This grave has been through the ages, in fact, the resort for patriots who were enraged. Bitter verses have been written on it:

Not a leaf to wave o'er that lonely grave
That seemed not a grave to me!
But a trench where some traitor was flung of yore—
'Tis a sight for a foeman's eye!
Where Patrick still and St. Columcille
And our Dove of the Oak Tree lie.

The reputed burial place of Patrick, Brigid and Columcille is a triumph of incongruity.

The further history of St. Brigid's remains brings us to Portugal. There is a story that three Irish knights set out for the Holy Land in the year 1283, that is, at a period when the crusading spirit was fast dying out in Europe. They carried with them from Ireland the head of St. Brigid. On their passage through Portugal, they apparently found friends and were induced to remain.

The full story of the three Irish knights is not known, but their treasure, St. Brigid's head, remained in Portugal. A stone set in the wall of the parish church of Lumiar, three miles outside Lisbon, records the coming of the knights and the fact that their bodies are interred within. The same church contains a chapel dedicated to St. Brigid, containing a statue of the saint, dressed in white. The relic has always been preserved in this church, which is one of the oldest in Lisbon, dating from the twelfth century.

A relic consisting of a portion of St. Brigid's skull was brought back from Lumiar in the year 1929 and enshrined in the new Church of St. Brigid in Killester, Dublin. There is a similar relic in St. James's Church, Killester; another in the parish church of Faughart; and another in the Convent of Mercy, Dundalk. There is in the National Museum, Dublin, a reliquary said to be that of her slipper.

It will be conceded that we cannot in Ireland venerate in any worthy fashion Brigid's earthly remains. One may state, without fear of giving offence, that no monument to her in this country expresses in a fitting manner her vast and enduring significance to the Irish race. But in direct contrast to the paucity of her relics, to the silence concerning her in stone, there are the profusion of traditions and the ardent, vehement devotion that is being forever proclaimed to her by the Irish people. The blank absence of the one is as chilling as the emphatic presence of the other is warm. If her people have not painted and carved and wrought and built in her honour, yet neither indeed have they forgotten. And in this respect the cult of St. Brigid of Ireland is one of the most sublime offerings ever laid at the feet of mortal woman, because, with so little material aid or external symbolism of any kind, it has burned with such ardour through fifteen hundred years, fed by the spirit only.

St. Brigid has never been honoured under the lofty dome of splendid cathedrals in her own land. The Irish people's conception of her has not been expressed in marble for the niches of palace walls; nor traced in delicate mosaics; nor painted in glowing frescoes; nor even enshrined in a literature through which genius might exalt her. Rather was it in mud cabins, or beside the Mass-rock in some wind-swept glen, or by fugitives, in concealment and flight, in underground caves, on emigrant ships, in the slave-gangs of the Barbadoes, in the basement kitchens of pagan cities, that she has been steadfastly honoured in the heart.

Her multitude of namesakes, decade after decade, have been flung from the shores of their own land like so much refuse, off-scourings of

exile, to become the accepted hewers of wood
and drawers of water, so that today the diminu-
tive Biddy stands in dictionaries of the English
language for the synonym of slavey, or menial.
But Brigid means strength, too, and this cor-
ruption of a name never extended to the soul.
Though all else was lost by the Biddies, some
rags of the dignity, some vestiges of the moral
splendour of St. Brigid ever clung to the bearers
of her name.

One would imagine that the Celtic saints
knew by divine prescience of the future testing,
so cunningly did they build the spiritual fabric,
so ruthless was their concentration on essen-
tials, so stark the spirit of abnegation they bred
in their disciples. One would imagine that they
had devised a special spiritual structure that
should weather those four hundred nightmare
years of religious persecution, and that long
cycle, even eight hundred years, of political
oppression. They even taught—those all-wise—
an independence of relics and of shrines, which
is a principle hardly encountered elsewhere. But
it would have gone hard with the Gael had his
trust been in shrines. When St. Ciaran was
dying, he said to his disciples:

> Hasten to other quiet places and leave my re-
> mains just like the dry bones of the stag on the
> mountain; for it is better that you should be

with my spirit in heaven than alongside my bones on earth with scandal.

It was from the Celtic saints that the Irish learned in what consists the perfect remembering. St. Francis of Assisi wrote in one of his poems:

Un arbore d'amore con gran frutto
In cor plantato mi da pasciemento.

(It is the most fruitful tree of love, planted in my heart, that gives me food.)

Such a tree of love did St. Brigid of Ireland plant in the heart of her people for all time, and it was upon this sustenance they fed. In the midst of what was an arid waste externally, the inner garden bloomed. The tree of love took vital root and assumed those graceful proportions that exalt the imagination. It blossomed to gladden the secret heart; gave shelter in the heat and stress of noonday; shed perfumes that refreshed; and bore fruit so potently sustaining, that the longest road round the world, the most arduous of missionary journeys, might well seem but that short step from the fields at Iona in the evening under the Abbot's benediction when labour was done.